Nike's Consumer Direct Offense, Amazon & StockX

The Disruption of Sneaker Retail

By Christopher D. Burns, MFA
Contributions by Tayib Salami

Books by Christopher D. Burns, MFA

One Hour to Wealth: Your Great Idea is Valuable; Get Up & Write It Down

The 30 Day Project: How Daily Dedication Can Lead to Something Amazing

F- -k Speeches & Inspiration: Where Do I Get the Money to Start?

Nike's Consumer Direct Offense, Amazon & StockX

The Disruption of Sneaker Retail

By Christopher D. Burns, MFA
Contributions by Tayib Salami

cbp
CB Publishing
2019

First Printing: 2019

ISBN 9781795704854

CB Publishing

www.cbpublish.com

www.arch-usa.com

www.housakicks.com

Ordering Information:

Special discounts are available on quantity purchases by corporations, associations, educators, and others. For details, contact the publisher at the above listed address.

U.S. trade bookstores and wholesalers: Please contact Christopher D. Burns at cdburns@cbpublish.com or visit www.arch-usa.com

Dedication

This book is dedicated to my family for putting up with the long phone calls with Tayib as we built the ARCH x Housakicks Network over the past four years.

What started as two guys who wanted to learn and share as much information as possible about the sneaker industry, became a business venture and a friendship that culminated in the writing of this book.

While I wrote the majority of the text the ideas generated via discussions with Tayib sparked the foundation of a book we think will give sneakerheads a bit more savvy in understanding the footwear industry and business in general; and will also help retailers and brands to find a means of connecting with fans and consumers.

Table of Contents

Foreword

This was not an easy book to write. Typically books on business have source or reference material. There are books on the sneaker industry, but they have primarily covered style, fashion and how and why sneakers have inspired an entire culture around shoes meant for the participation in sports.

I didn't have the ability to refer to another text. Most of the information found in this book was derived from my work in the sneaker industry over the last 15 years; so there are sections that deal directly with my own experiences. My 'sneaker career' began with the development of two small sneaker companies.

Sho-Shot was my first company. I operated the business from 2005 to 2008 via a license with a group based in Canada. Under my watch I got the uniforms for the company onto 9 colleges and sold 1200 pair of shoes using a grassroots approach. As I began to really find my way the owner of the license took the company and shifted into a different direction. I was stuck without a brand I had built for three years.

I launched ARCH, *Athletes Require Competition and Heart*, in 2009. I took the experiences I learned from Sho-Shot and from 2009 to 2016 I sold over 600 pair of shoes with six different styles and over 20 different colorways. I only had one employee during this time and while the work I did was admirable, it was extremely difficult. I lost over 30,000 dollars during the operation of the brand, but I also ran a successful Kickstarter in 2014 to stave off the end of the brand. I guess the question you might be asking is "how I could afford to lose 30,000 and still operate ARCH?" During the process of running both Sho-Shot and ARCH I was also one of the first 'resellers' in Memphis. I initially set up shop at a local flea market where fake sneakers were sold. The owner of the flea market placed my booth in the front because I had receipts and I was the only seller in the market with real shoes. The rest of the market was operated out of shipping containers where the sellers had thousands of knock offs. Because I was also a tenure track college professor I only set up on the weekends with my own brand and the sneakers I was picking up from local stores. Here is the crazy thing about working out of the flea market, people would ask me the price of my shoes and they didn't care that I had real shoes. They could walk to the multitude of guys in the back of the market selling fakes and get three pair for 100 bucks. I was selling one pair for 100 bucks. I would make around 500 to 1000 dollars a weekend. The guys selling fakes would be making 3000 to 5000 dollars a weekend. When I launched ARCH I also began selling online. The summers were brutal at the market and the winters weren't much better. As my eBay store began to grow and I was making almost as much as I earned as an educator, I decided to start transitioning away from the flea market and education.

In 2011 the flea market was raided. The DEA, Homeland Security, ICE, and the USPS Service had built up cases around the shipments of fakes coming into the market. The sellers were selling knock off purses, shoes and luxury items. The flea market was shut down, and this coincided with my eBay store being shut down. I discuss this later in the book. After eBay I moved to Amazon's Marketplace and what I learned there is the foundation of this book.

All of my experiences led to a redesign of my business in 2015. While most analysts and consultants in the sneaker industry have worked for a brand or a retail chain, I have worked outside of the structure. All of the relationships I made with store owners, managers and district managers in this region gave me insight into the sneaker industry, all of the grey areas I've operated in, the launch of shoe companies, importing, designing, all of the experiences I've been through makes for a very interesting read.

As I said, this was not an easy book to write and it isn't easy to read. It wanders in and out of point of views and is both personal and business writing. It's like a good sneaker closet, casual, athletic, stylish and purposeful. I thank you for picking the book up.

Chapter

1 Introduction

When *Rapper's Delight* released in 1979 everybody I knew went crazy. Old people danced because they thought it was *Good Times by Chic*, and younger people liked the rhyming. I was a little kid, and I went crazy. It was the same when I heard *Punk Rock Rap* by the Cold Crush Brothers. It was the same when I bought a tape with the song *Planet Rock* that included a "How to Breakdance" poster. I found some cardboard and went outside to try to do backspins. When I first saw *Beat Street* I had to go to the one kid in the neighborhood's house who had cable. After that movie I spent every penny I could scrape so I could look like 'Lee' in the film. When I saw Grandmaster Flash's video for *You Know What Time It Is* the song became the foundation of how I wrote graffiti and to this day I still use the same style when I draw my name on a wall. I use chalk because I'm hanging with my daughter, but you get what I'm saying. After watching *Beat Street* I begged my mom for a pair of Pumas. I didn't get them. I ended up with a pair of Kangaroos with the pouch on the side. Walter Payton wore Roos so I wasn't out of style, it just didn't make sense for me to be wearing a pair of Astroturf football shoes to play basketball in. I didn't want those shoes and the universe took over and made things happen.

I was playing in an area we called the woods and stepped on a nail. The blood from the nail going through my foot ruined the shoes. I didn't think about the fact that I couldn't walk, I just knew I wouldn't have to rock Roos anymore. I finally got a pair of Puma… and they were turfs also. I eventually got a pair of Nike Air, and I wore a hole into those shoes and then *Run DMC* happened. After Run DMC all I wore was adidas. All of these things happened before I hit 13 years old. By the time I got my first job at 16 as a stockboy at a small grocery store, I had been forced to wear Pro Wings that looked like the Air Jordan 1. My mom had to keep my sneakers on the porch because they smelled like death, although they looked fresh because I changed the shoe strings in them, they were still bobos, but when I finally got my first pair of adidas… those stayed fresh and I had several pair that I could rotate. My sister was in the Navy and sent me adidas jogging suits. I had adidas shirts that looked like the old Coca Cola logo shirts. Everything I wore was adidas. I can find five different pictures from my high school years and in those pics I have on a different pair of adidas. Everyone else had on Jordans or Dunks or Converse Weapons. I have always been into sneakers since before there was a thing called *sneaker culture* or *sneakerheads*.

I bring this up to state that those teens who listened to *Rapper's Delight* are in their 40s and 50s. They are the ones who transitioned sneakers from "gym" shoes to fashion. Yeah, the Converse Chuck Taylor was being worn by rock and punk bands, but it wasn't until Hip-Hop made basketball sneakers fashionable that sneaker companies began to experience explosive growth. I can take this one step more and state that even Nike was stagnant until they pulled off a coup in signing a gold chain wearing, high flying, 360 degree dunking… wait a minute that's Darryl Dawkins... Nike was on the verge of bankruptcy when the brand signed another gold chain wearing, high flying basketball player named Michael Jordan, who hated Hip-Hop, but was Hip-Hop. Nike changed everything. That gold chain wearing basketball player could have also been George "Iceman" Gervin. Gervin didn't dunk though, he *finger rolled*, but he was the star of one of the greatest posters in marketing from Nike. The poster where the Iceman was sitting on a throne made out of ice. No one had really highlighted basketball players like Nike did. There was a Moses Malone poster as well. All of them had the Nike logo in the corner. When Michael Jordan took off in his red and black track suit the sneaker wars began.

Nike took what could be considered elements of Hip-Hop in basketball and sneakers and turned it into a billion dollar business. In marketing basketball Nike found a blueprint for other marketing avenues and this helped to lead the company out of a moment where they were laying off employees. Basketball changed everything. Athletes had always represented the brand, but Michael Jordan delivered a schematic and Nike followed it up with Bo Jackson and Cross Training, Andre Agassi and tennis commercials, and more basketball with Charles Barkley in a commercial with Public Enemy rapping. Hip-Hop made it okay to wear sneakers as casual wear.

In 2018 the retro trend resurrected brands like Fila and Champion. If the street/Hip-Hop/counter culture element was removed from the sneaker industry today, the retro trend would be dead. Actually, the sneaker industry would be crippled because people would only buy shoes that they need and not the shoes that allow them to capture some aspect of cool. Nike wouldn't have to create countless colors. Puma wouldn't have Rihanna, and adidas wouldn't make Yeezys. Every brand would make *all white* and *all black* shoes and there wouldn't be signature models or shoes made by rappers. The sneaker industry as it is today wouldn't exist and by extension the luxury market, Gucci, Louis Vuitton, would be a fledgling segment, but that's another discussion.

The *sneakerhead* community is often considered an isolated, niche market; a bunch of pimply faced, teenage boys who go to conventions to barter, buy and trade. The reality is sneaker culture began in the 70s when B-Boys and Girls began taking shoes created for basketball (The Puma Clyde) to break (breakdance) in, or simply to get *fresh.* As footwear began to develop and grow shifting from performance to fashion and casual wear, somewhere along the way the term *sneakerhead* arrived.

Who coined the phrase sneakerhead? I can't find a definitive answer, but Bobbito Garcia[1] was the first to really address the culture in his book *Where'd You Get Those*. In that book he had this quote, "We were the first generation, and only one, to enjoy sneaker consumption on our own terms." The term really came into play in the 90's and took off in the 2000's. What most people have come to think about in regard to sneakerheads is that these people are collectors and pursue limited release models and obscure styles. What I consider a sneakerhead is any person who grew up with a desire to have the coolest pair of kicks. This creates a broad spectrum and places everyone in the realm of *sneakerhead*. My description makes it complicated to apply analysis. It expands the reach of sneakerheads; which is necessary because I think sneakerheads are more influential than people realize.

---

[1] Bobbito Garcia is Hip-Hop's DaVinci. He is a DJ, writer, film maker, designer and has created some of the best basketball related street events. He was the first to have a show all about sneakers on ESPN and his radio show with DJ Stretch Armstrong was at the forefront of the Golden Era of Hip-Hop. Sneaker culture wouldn't exist as it is without Kool Bob Love.

Sneaker culture has become mainstream. A quick search online garners report after report on reselling sneakers and articles on how athleisure is driving fashion. One look at the income of major sneaker companies now vs the year 2000 and there is a direct correlation to the rise of the NBA which is also synonymous with the rise of Hip-Hop culture. Here is the annual revenue of the biggest sneaker companies in 2017/2018:

Nike's annual revenue = 34.5 Billion dollars

adidas' annual revenue = 24.4 Billion dollars

Here are the annual revenues of Nike and adidas in 2000:

Nike's annual revenue = 8.9 Billion dollars

adidas' annual revenue = 5 Billion dollars

When you consider Michael Jordan's ascent in the 90s took place at the same time that rap music began to dominate radio and television. By the time MJ retired in the early 2000s sneaker brands had players like Allen Iverson and Kobe Bryant on their rosters. The NBA had to create a dress code to prevent players from dressing like Hip-Hop artists. Basketball had become an international sport with the original Dream Team, but And1[2] took basketball from the gym to the Street and gave rise to a "Venom" styled symbiotic relationship between hoops and Hip-Hop. Rappers wanted to be basketball players (Master P) and ballers wanted to be rappers (Shaq, Kobe and Allen Iverson all had rap albums). Reebok gave Jay Z and 50 Cent sneaker deals and Allen Iverson appeared in commercials with Jadakiss. This relationship remains today bolstered by streetwear and rappers like Kanye West, Drake and Pharrell, with Rihanna completely turning around the fortunes of Puma.

What does all of this have to do with Nike and their direct to consumer strategy known as *Consumer Direct Offense*? Everything. There may be someone reading this who is asking, "Are people really that obsessed with sneakers?" There may be someone reading this asking, "Can anything about sneaker culture and the sneaker business

---

[2] And1 was a brand created by Seth Berger in 1993. The company initially sold a face-less logo tee with trash talking on the shirts. The brand developed into a traveling basketball team of streetballers who played at legendary courts like The Rucker. The brand landed an ESPN show and the And1 game was forever tied with Hip-Hop. And1 launched sneakers that landed on the feet of NBA players and holds a place in one of the most important dunks in the history of the league, Vince Carter's elbow in the rim dunk during the 2000 NBA Slam Dunk Contest.

be compared to other industries?" The answer is yes to both questions.

I gave a very short history of sneakers to establish that the growth of the business moves with cultural shifts in art, sport and lifestyle. Right now in 2019 we are within another shift rooted in the digital world. Music is now streamed. Sneakers are bought with a phone, and kids would rather be an eSports athlete instead of an NBA athlete. The NBA has even created its own eSports franchises. The digital shift is unlike anything business, notice I didn't say sneaker business, has ever experienced. To understand where retail is headed it's important to look at the past.

I wrote that last section because there is a lot of business writing coming and I wanted to ease you into this discussion. Let's get into it.

Chapter 2

Money Is On the Table

As the years pass, shifts in shopping take place. The history of sneaker retail is littered with the remains of mom and pop shops. This is understood. What isn't being focused on today, however, is the impact digital has had on the sneaker retail industry. Wall Street and every analyst is well aware of Amazon and how the tentacles of the company are reaching into every facet of life, but there is a lack of attention being paid to how brands have been made solvent without the need to enter into more wholesale agreements. This has left traditional retail in a difficult position. One that I don't think is being clearly presented.

This book was originally a problem and solution discussion on why brick and mortar retail needs to focus on creating more active, content based websites to engage consumers. After spending 2018 doing a comparison of e-commerce third party platforms for reselling sneakers, I realized that a more detailed analysis was needed. I couldn't write a book just about building more engaging websites with content, I had to address how Nike's direct to consumer strategy and third party sneaker websites have disrupted traditional retail. I had to present evidence that the athletic footwear and apparel industry is in an era unlike any time in the history of sneaker retail. I hope the multi-faceted approach in this book doesn't create confusion. The book reads like a website/social feed where there is primary content in the middle of the page and two sidebars inviting you to click through to other information.

I've written a lot of this book based on discussions with Tayib Salami who is my business partner in the AHN (ARCH x Housakicks Network) websites. The book consists of information derived from my extensive experience in Third Party Resale and as the owner of two footwear brands. Another aspect of this book derives from the data created by sneaker sales where I utilized a pureplay third party platform that was begun in 2016; StockX and Tayib used a combination of older e-commerce sites in Kixify, eBay and his own Housakicks website.

My goal is threefold (that's a rhyme).

1. I will discuss Nike's Consumer Direct Offense and how the strategy is as disruptive a force in sneaker retail as anything the industry has seen.
2. I will discuss sneaker culture websites and their influence on how buyers discover and shop for products. I will also talk about third party online e-commerce sites and how the sites were born from Amazon and eBay, but have become multimillion dollar websites garnering considerable investments. I'll explain that both sneaker lifestyle sites and sneaker resale sites exist because they focus more on content around sneaker culture than the traditional retail/wholesale accounts that carry sneakers.

3. I will show that a considerable amount of money is being left on the table by both brands and retailers.

Bringing these elements together in this book will not be easy. It will take a lot of transitions, but I hope that the business world and sneaker culture will read this and find information that informs, drives discussion and creates opportunity.

Chapter 3

The Apple Play

What exactly does a brick and mortar retailer need to continue growth and expansion in a world that has moved towards online sales? Stores such as *Sheikh*, which recently entered bankruptcy and discharged in 2018, and *The Sports Authority*, which completed bankruptcy and has been closed, show the limitations of retail. Chains such as *The Athlete's Foot,* which has disappeared, and the merger of *Villa and DTLR*[3] establish that sneaker/urban retail are not the fast growth areas they once were. Brick and mortar sneaker retailers attempting to grow are entering a time unlike any other in the history of footwear.

[3] In 2017 the two companies merged creating a 230 store business. They operate in what is considered 'urban' retail.

As brands become more focused on driving engagement with the consumer to gain a larger share of sales directly to the traditional shopper, this shapes retail and is unlike anything traditional retail has had to face before. The move by brands can be considered what I term the "Apple Play". Sneaker companies are beginning to function like online startups who have watched Apple go from a brand on the brink of failure to a trillion dollar corporation[4] with their own showrooms. Apple's direct-to-consumer 'startup environment' has created a disruption for traditional *computer* retail in both the brick and mortar and e-commerce space. The *Apple Play* can be described by taking a close look at how Apple launched their brick and mortar locations. Apple created a curated, personalized shopping experience. Their system included a **Genius Bar**, for computer repair in store; **Apple Concierge**, a new name for sales leads, and **One to One** trainers: Concierge who have been trained to work independently with customers who signed up for the service by the same name. Apple Concierge/sales leads, over ten years ago, had handheld devices to complete transactions at any moment during a customer's discovery. Customers could literally check out in any section of the store. The mobile checkout

[4] https://www.bloomberg.com/graphics/2018-apple-at-one-trillion-market-cap/

capitalized on the emotional experience of visiting the Apple Store to play with the variety of products. The only difference between Apple and Sneaker Retail is that Apple has a very limited product range; which has not stopped Apple from becoming one of the biggest companies in the world. I state this because sneaker retail is in the precarious position of providing "newness" on a weekly basis. This does not have to be the case if retailers control their narrative beyond simply presenting the product, which moves this discussion too far ahead.

Apple enhanced the *in-store* experience with **One to One** instructors, which created another stream of revenue for the company. When I worked at Apple in 2007 *One to One* provided individual assistance to customers who signed up. Apple discontinued *One to One* in favor of "Workshops" in 2015. Nike has obviously looked to Apple for a source of ideas. Tim Cook has been on Nike's board for years, but in 2016 Apple's Tim Cook became the Lead Independent Director on Nike's board[5]. The current Consumer Direct Offense (Nike's strat-

[5] http://fortune.com/2016/06/30/apple-ceo-tim-cook-nike/

egy formally introduced during Investor's Day 2017) has Apple's fingerprints all over it.

At Apple the *in-store* job promotions to *One to One instructors*, added levels that could be attained by sales leads. *One to One* instructors eventually could become 'Genius level', handling repair. The *in-store* levels created opportunity beyond the traditional structure of retail (sales lead, storeroom, assistant manager, manager). This new structure for employees coupled with an increase in pay for those at the bottom of the retail employment chain created a commitment to Apple by sales leads, this is something severely needed in sneaker retail as sales leads have a high turnover rate which creates considerable issues at all footwear stores.

The *Apple Play* is at the root of every brand (Nike, adidas, etc.) launching new retail options (online and brick and mortar). During quarterly reports for every sneaker company one of the largest areas of growth is in DTC (Direct to Consumer). Nike created the term **Consumer Direct Offense** to explain their DTC. In their *Investor's Day 2017* they made the statement that in the US they would control 80% of the distribution of their footwear. This is a similar move to Apple. Apple still has some wholesale relationships, but Apple product is primarily sold via Apple doors; removing the need to rely solely on wholesale to generate revenue.

For publicly traded sportswear companies, the increase in margins from DTC drives shareholder loyalty, which allows for the capital that generates the innovation connecting brands to consumers. Nike's recent increase in shareholder value has coincided with the introduction of new technologies, both sports advancements and digital technology. But why are brands really implementing the *Apple Play*? What created an environment where a company like Nike, that was built on *Futures,* has completely removed the Futures model as evidence of company growth?

(In the J.B. Strasser book *Swoosh*, Futures were described as a way for Nike to create cashflow and get hard commitments on shoe orders months ahead of delivery.)

Chapter 4

Intentional Disruption?

The promotional environment at retail, which has been in a 4+ year cycle, aligns with a few different instances that created opportunities for Nike. Opportunities were available for other brands, but only adidas surged in sales initially and then smaller brands like Fila and Vans captured a share of the retro market.

One of those promotional instances was with MSRP[6] guidelines. As MSRP wasn't enforced as much (brands had to approve of looser guidelines for MSRP), more and more *on sale* product began showing up in the market. Smaller chains implemented outlets (to re-

[6] Manufacturer's Suggested Retail Price is how much a brand requests that their shoes price point should be. Nike traditionally didn't allow retailers to advertise Nike products being "on sale".

move inventory and create room in the back of house), but the outlet model has not been effective. The reduction in SRP has been diminishing the sell through of new release product.

Here is a hypothetical situation: What if Nike purposefully contributed to creating a promotional environment with the intent of removing struggling/small accounts? If Nike is opening more doors and attempting to go direct to consumer they could have intentionally flooded the market with product on *Futures* styled scheduling and utilized the RTV[7] system to stock their own stores. (The reality is Nike's CDO was a means of controlling costs and inventory.)

Consider this, when both The Sports Authority and Sheikh applied for bankruptcy, both companies owed Nike millions of dollars. The footwear from The Sports Authority was *rtv'd* to Nike's Factory and Clearance Stores. Where traditionally outlets were the home to footwear and apparel from previous seasons, some Nike Clearance and Factory Stores now carry the same releases that are being sold on launch day in retail stores.

---

[7] Return to vendor

At a local level, small accounts disappeared. One small chain I visited simply could not afford to purchase more inventories because as the owner shared, "Nike increased the number of shoes and the amount of apparel that had to be purchased for an account to get the premium best-selling Jordan retro products."

From 2012 to the present Nike has opened over 100 additional stores. Nike is challenging the entire sneaker industry because Footlocker is one of the only companies with more brick and mortar locations that carry the Swoosh. This is telling and can be considered proof of Nike's intent to create an *Apple styled* system. If Nike continues to add doors, what prevents other brands from following suit? Many retailers believe that Nike will always need them because of the cash customer. There is a danger in this train of thought because it relies on the old system of wholesale and retail and Apple completely changed the way the game is played. Apple utilizes mobile carriers as *Operating System Delivery Platforms* for their phones and some retail for their computers, but Apple stores are the showrooms. In other words, you can buy an Apple product from a business like T-Mobile or AT&T, but the contract requires the owner to utilize Apple's cloud and storage features. In order to update your phone you must be signed in to an Apple account. Cash customers have iPhones. If the cash customer is one of the primary users of smartphones and the smartphone is shaping retail, making the mistake of thinking that the cash customer will remain a buoy is comparable to Blockbuster thinking DVD rental would always be a form of entertainment.

Nike is advancing the changes in the footwear industry in a very similar fashion. They have explained that "inside of their digital platforms consumers purchase three times more than they typically would[8]." The moat of the cash customer is a barrier that has a bridge and it's not just Nike attempting to find a way across to the dollars there. Amazon is finding a way as well; which will be discussed later.

I asked the question, "What if Nike's CDO was intentional disruption?" If I sell a business a product and I understand that they are slow in making their payments, the logical approach would be to allow that store to adjust so that they won't struggle and they can continue to purchase products once the business is back on steady

---

[8] https://arch-usa.com/2017-nike-inc-investor-meeting-the-scale-of-sport-highlights-a-detailed-breakdown/

ground, right? Nike hasn't done this with their wholesale accounts. If the account is not capable of making their payments Nike continued to deliver the product to the stores. This would have been okay if the product Nike was delivering wasn't overproduced and creating an inventory nightmare.

Smaller Nike retail locations and larger locations were allowed to RTV. These return to vendors allowed Nike to fill their stores, but the accounts with Nike couldn't afford to take on more product. Nike could then close that account because the store simply couldn't keep up.

If a company with the bestselling product requests that an account redesign their store and take on more product that isn't as coveted to continue getting move coveted product, that's like Shaq *dropstepping* on a point guard. It's bully basketball, but it's also genius. If a store gains more product and it has all of the channels for sales being operated: an active website with a solid e-commerce platform, engaging content to drive traffic, solid social media and in-store loyalty programs, more product should be a bonus. The problem is most retailers aren't hitting on all cylinders. What may have been an intentional push by Nike could be explained as giving an account what they wanted (more product) and the account simply failed to execute. It's an interesting discussion.

Nike's digital adjustments are creating opportunities for disruption. When a company that was built on wholesale decides to go directly to their consumer, there are holes that need to be filled both inside of physical stores and in e-commerce. The issue is sneaker retail has been slow to respond in filling these holes. One of the few companies that adjusted quickly was Foot Locker. As Nike delivered a ton of product that underperformed, Foot Locker shifted their stores to brands that showed improvement. I created a term called the *Nike wall* to explain companies so reliant on Nike that they failed to give real estate to other brands. This reliance on the Nike wall means the companies with the most on-hand inventory saw the loosening of MSRP guidelines from Nike as an opportunity; when in reality the discounted pricing opened the stores up to disruption… from internet based third party platforms.

Chapter

5

The Birth of 3rd Party Sneaker Shops

The rise of Amazon and eBay contributed to a factor many retail businesses do not seem to be discussing. "Warby Parker-esque" online e-tailers/third party sellers have grown over the last 14 years as direct descendants of Amazon and eBay[9]. A small brand in the sneaker industry like Greats has been able to grow because online has been established as a solid way to introduce a brand. Third party sellers on Amazon and eBay have fueled a fast growing resell business that was originally operated out of retail chains.

---

[9] Warby Parker is an online company founded in 2010 that disrupted the eyeglass market.

Third party buyers used to directly support stores like DTLR, Jimmy Jazz and even Foot Locker. As Nike has opened more locations, the brand has added a new component to the inventory sold by third party merchants.

As *sneakerhead* culture grew and became mainstream, the appetite for kicks grew, not just for kids willing to camp overnight and line up for shoes; everybody began to utilize sneakers in daily wear creating explosive growth in the industry. The everyday use of sneakers as footwear outside of performance is directly linked to the rise of Hip-Hop and the influence of the NBA on kids who traded in Sebagos and penny loafers for basketball shoes. Sneaker releases became regional and often a new basketball shoe couldn't be found in some local stores. This moved sneakerheads to messageboards online where people were able to help each other find kicks. This was the original third party resale.

Third party sellers purchase footwear at retail and resell the shoes at a modest margin. Those margins grew as more people entered the online shopping arena and online stores began to make millions. This was good for the sneaker ecosystem as buyers helped retail outlets clear inventory. The problem is the third party marketplace created false positives for retailers that compounded an issue overlooked by many stores.

When a reseller buys a particular item at a chain the system shows an increase in sales on particular styles. Those stores then receive an increase of styles that may no longer hold the same value. This creates a surplus in inventory. Which contributes to mark downs and begins the promotional cycle. Resale is not based on data; resale is based on hype which is qualitative.

Many of the sellers that make and have made Amazon and eBay two of the largest online sellers of footwear are now being supported by Nike/Brand stores. The Memphis area has three Nike stores. These stores are comparable to the seven local Foot Locker stores simply based on the square footage of the Nike Factory and Clearance Store. The third Nike Store in Memphis is an Employee Store which creates a completely different issue for local retailers and for e-commerce.

The online retailers that initially began on eBay and Amazon are no longer simply "third party resellers". These pureplay online *businesses* are garnering considerable investments and some are transitioning to brick and mortar. I italicized 'business' because resale, although very lucrative on a small scale, is not a business. At any point stores could quickly identify 'resellers' and blacklist those people. The problem is many brick and mortar stores lack the agility of the third party marketplace, which means that they can't reach the consumer. This leaves an opening for resale to take place.

While third party resale is only a small portion of sales in the footwear market, the belief that it has not and is not creating issues for traditional retail is a serious oversight. Businesses like Stadium Goods, Campless (which was a blog and grew into StockX and will be discussed in great detail later), GOAT, an app that recently purchased Flight Club[10] Stores, allowing the app to transition into brick and mortar, and BAIT, which now has 7 locations and is looking to expand even more, have long been a thorn in the side of traditional retail's online growth. More important, these online businesses have

---

[10] Flight Club is a consignment based sneaker and streetwear shop with brick and mortar locations and a solid online presence.

attracted over 200 million dollars in investments. Websites that once worked to simply report and share information on the sneaker industry are now being publicly traded on stock markets. Hypebeast, a blog originally, is publicly traded in China. The blog has launched Hypebae and HBX. HBX.com, an online retailer for Hypebeast, is hitting 1 million visits a month; doubling the monthly visits of brick and mortar chains like Sneaker Politics, City Gear and DTLR.

Sole Collector is a news website that is a part of a network of sneaker sites for Complex (including Weartesters and SneakerNews). Complex was recently acquired by Verizon Hearst in a 100 million dollar + investment. Sole Collector recently launched **Slang** an online platform for sneaker sales. Kicks On Fire, a sneaker blog, has owned **Kixify** for over six years; the owner was featured on a Forbes 30 Under 30 list. Kixify is an online marketplace for sneakers. Kixify garners nearly a million visits per month. Stadium Goods does not have an account with Nike[11], but still has had impressive growth and of these third party resellers they are shipping internationally allowing them to expand. They had one of the biggest days in the history of

---

[11] https://arch-usa.com/stadium-goods-continues-to-push-the-concept-of-sneaker-reselling-sneaker-investments/

Single's Day in China. Stadium Goods recently was invested into by luxury fashion brand Louis Vuitton. Mark Cuban also dropped 4.6 million into Stadium Goods. They are moving towards expansion into more brick and mortar locations. StockX was a blog (Campless.com) that garnered an investment from Cleveland Cavaliers owner Dan Gilbert. The site has quickly become one of the most visited websites in footwear in less than 2 years. The company recently had a funding round of 40 Million dollars and will be hiring an additional 1000 employees and they have expanded into Europe[12]. In 2018 I spent an entire year reselling sneakers through the platform full time. This means that I would operate my website and then spend time every day analyzing StockX's market to make acquisitions to buy and sell. The result by the end of the year holds invaluable evidence of the amount of money being left on the table by sneaker retail. The year of sales also establishes that much of retail has failed to adapt to how and why online shoppers visit websites. I will dive into this in another section.

Why would I take the time to list these online businesses? Stadium Goods and other online resale platforms basically 'operated' out

12 https://arch-usa.com/stockx-continues-to-bring-in-big-funding-rounds-44m-investment-to-hire-1000-employees/

of stores like City Gear and DTLR. These are sellers who don't have wholesale accounts with brands. The product that is being sold is arriving via consignment or being directly purchased from physical locations. Many of the online stores were initially stores on Amazon and eBay, or simply websites. The businesses in the last paragraph that began as blogs (HBX, Kixify) have built in audiences that traditional retail can't reach. Actually it's not that they can't reach those audiences, they are relying on the moat of the cash customer and the perceived value of instant gratification. When you consider Hibbett Sports didn't have an e-commerce platform until a year ago, and it is a major chain, it becomes obvious that traditional retail hasn't really paid attention to the third party online platforms. This can be seen in a quick check of online traffic.

At this point the only retail chain attracting the traffic that StockX is getting online is Footlocker and its derivatives. This is a prediction: although Nike has claimed to be removing accounts, the digital footprint of these e-tailers suggests that they will all eventually become tiered sellers of Nike products especially as they shift into brick and mortar, or they will all work with Nike in some fashion.

The digital footprint of third party online retail is a disruption to the online growth of traditional retailers. It is important that chains begin to take the time to analyze the impending battlefront. I'm not stating that chains like City Gear, EbLens, and DTLR are not aware. I want to make it clear that decisions will have to be made to take the battle *to* e-commerce platforms while fighting to maintain the fragile relationship with brands focused on selling their own products.

Chapter 6

Sneaker Website Traffic

In the previous section I listed e-commerce/pureplay sites that are disrupting retailer's e-commerce growth. The following list shows the monthly website traffic of sites in the sneaker business. Not included here are smaller sites like my own ARCH x Housakicks Network (AHN) which generates 500,000 to 1 Million dollars per year via ad and affiliate revenue and sneaker resale. This **Total Monthly Visits** list shows the dominance of Nike in digital. This list also gives an overview of how competitive the space is.

Total Monthly Visits (data compiled using Similarweb)

Nike.com **77.3 Million**

Complex.com 22.6 Million (Includes Solecollector.com 2.92 Million (Recently launched Slang Marketplace, sneakernews.com 6.06 Million, weartesters.com 989,000) Total = **32.58 Million**

Footlocker.com 15.95 Million (affiliated sites Footaction.com 1.29 Million, champsports.com 3.85 Million, eastbay.com 6.24 Million and Kidsfootlocker.com 2.53 Million) Total = **29.86 Million**

adidas.com **20.72 Million**

Hypebeast.com **13.43 Million** (subsite hbx.com 867,000) Total = **14.30 Million** (recently IPO'd)

Underarmour.com **9.85 Million**

Finishline.com **9.51 Million**

StockX.com **3.21 Million** (startup formerly campless.com) in 2017 StockX was at 3.21 Million visits per month. They are now at **10 Million+.**

Jimmyjazz.com **2.47 Million**

Kixify.com **1.56 Million**

Hibbett.com **1.11 Million** (Recently launched their ecommerce in 2017) In 2018 the site is garnering **2.41 Million**.

Citygear.com **431,000 (sold to Hibbett Sports in 2018)**

DTLR.com **258,000 (merged with Villa)**

sneakervilla.com **>12,000**

Since 2012 Nike has been implementing their *direct to consumer* agenda. The Swoosh did this in such a subversive manner that analysts monitoring the brand for the stock market did not realize the moves the brand was making. It did not become apparent what Nike's end game was until October of 2017. In their Investor's Day event labeled "The Scale of Sport[13]", the brand gave a complete breakdown of how their **Consumer Direct Offense** would lead the company to 50Billion per year revenue. For years the Nike *direct to consumer* strategy did not have a name. To be honest no one was writing about it except ARCH. I took notice in 2012. Although I wasn't writing about it on my ARCH site, I studied all footwear companies because I was operating ARCH. I was designing, importing and releasing my own sneakers. A quick glance at my website will show reports on the strategies I was implementing to reach the consumer. It was my work

[13] https://arch-usa.com/2017-nike-inc-investor-meeting-the-scale-of-sport-highlights-a-detailed-breakdown/

on ARCH (my footwear company, not the site) that led to a more in-depth understanding of Amazon's brand registry and Amazon's Ad Program. I combined the information I had to learn with information I read and studied on Nike and on retail websites. As I released my third shoe in 2012 I was also looking into how I could land a deal with Foot Locker potentially. What I discovered was that Foot Locker had been increasing their share of the online sales market. It made perfect sense that this was the case as the chain was really the first to dive into an online strategy. Zappos was really the best digital platform for footwear sales and they were acquired by Amazon, but that's not the point I'm making here. Foot Locker, who had shown considerable online growth, began to see a slowdown in online sales. This happened as Nike began to make a concentrated effort on digital.

In October 2017, Nike delivered their manifesto and within the presentation they explained how they were limiting the number of retail partners. Wall Street responded negatively to Nike no longer using *Futures* as a metric for growth in 2016. I wrote several articles explaining that Wall Street was getting it wrong. For me everything became clear; Nike had successfully launched a strategy with an entire market unaware of what was to come.

I wrote this in response to a Wall Street analysis:

> This is a big part of why Wall Street doesn't get Nike's approach; they are valuating Nike on old standards of wholesale and retail. They aren't analyzing the *Warby Parkers* of the world who have launched online and shifted into multichannel and seen incredible growth. Nike works like a startup. Nike understands the importance of content creation for the next generation of sneaker consumers. This is why they paid Ronaldo so much money. This is why Nike is the only major sneaker company to actively launch several Content Management System based websites under the Nike Umbrella. SNKRS and Air.Jordan.Com are only the start as I can see Nike creating a fully functional media company that creates content for YouTube and eventually its own *television stations* for Nike events. Think about the way colleges are causing ESPN to fail

> by launching their own sports networks. Do you think Nike isn't paying attention? I mean if Hypebeast and Complex are considered multimillion dollar websites based on sneaker blogs, and Nike has launched sneaker blogs in SNKRS and Air.Jordan.Com don't think for a second that they are not contemplating a larger media approach for their DTC strategy.

When I wrote the above response to a Wall Street analyst *Breaking2* had not taken place. Breaking2 was a livestreamed event hosted on Twitter. The event took place on a race track in Italy. Nike's goal was to introduce their new running technology *Zoom X*[14]. Nike recruited three world class runners attempting to run a sub 2 hour marathon. I watched and actually livestreamed during the event to capture the number of people watching *Breaking2* on Twitter and the engagement was incredible. I wrote this during the event, "Traditional television sports viewing has fallen

---

[14] Nike ZoomX is lighter, softer and more responsive than any Nike foam, designed to maximize speed by delivering greater energy return. ZoomX was derived from a foam traditionally used in aerospace innovation, applied for the first time in performance footwear in the Nike Zoom Vaporfly Elite and 4%.

and right now there are so many people tweeting and watching this event that every second there are about 5 tweets."[15]

This livestream was the predecessor to Nike's *LeBron Watch.* LeBron Watch (2018) was the name of the release of limited sneakers via the Nike App during NBA games. When LeBron hit the floor in a particular pair of shoes those with the Nike App were notified that they could purchase shoes that would only release via the App. This was important as Nike disclosed that customers shopping inside of their Apps spent three times as much as visitors to the site.

Nike's CDO cannot be denied. Nike has found their Amazon 1 Click. The brand has found a way to get people to buy via their platform in the most effective way possible and it does not require a person to walk into a mall or store. This doesn't mean Nike is ignoring omnichannel opportunities. Nike's Factory and Clearance Stores are seeing similar increases in foot traffic and

[15] https://arch-usa.com/breaking2-is-an-amazing-event-nike-zoomx/

their Nike Athletes are now being measured on the number of sign-ups for Nike.com they acquire in store.

Nike's CDO was on display when the brand launched a Flash Sale for 50% off in 2017. While analysts were claiming that Nike was in trouble and they had never seen Nike do such a thing, because I had transcribed the Investor's Day I immediately saw this Flash Sale as a means of capturing new customers inside of the Nike App and Websites where the brand could add more customers to their sales environment where they have proven that people buy more. Analysts saw Nike's "inventory" issues as a problem. I said that Nike's inventory issues still earned them money on RTVs (return to vendors from wholesale accounts):

> **The Flash Sale is a marketing tactic which drives engagement on Nike's platform, and gives customers the perception they are getting an awesome deal.**
>
> Does Nike have too much inventory? OF COURSE!!!! They overproduced in the process of building DTC. Nike took on more RTVs as they wiped out smaller accounts. These RTVs are in their warehouses and stores; it has to be liquidated, and if you look at the prices on the Flash Sale you can break down the pricing as follows:

Kobe AD NXT

Retail: $200.00

Nike Flash Sale: $109.97

If Nike sold the Kobe to Foot Locker at wholesale the cost would be about 50% off of Retail or $100.00. Nike's Flash sale actually makes the brand almost the same amount of money than selling to a wholesale account.

Now let's look at a low end shoe.

Nike Roshe Two

Retail: $90.00

Nike Flash Sale: $44.97

If Nike sold this shoe wholesale they would get $49.50. In this instance the production cost of the Roshe is probably at $35.00 per pair. The margin on this shoe at $44.97 after shipping is razor thin, but if the product sells they can now apply **Edit to Amplify** and no longer produce that model. (Edit to Amplify was introduced in 2016 by Nike as a strategy to only produce models that have a strong sell through.)

The most important aspect to consider here is Nike is pulling an Amazon. A flash sale will attract visitors who would traditionally shop online with Amazon. Once a customer logs in and sets up an account on NDC, Nike can now add a new customer to their e-mail list and market directly to that customer. When

> you consider that brands have to spend on influencers, social media ads and Google ads to drive traffic to their online platform, Nike's announcement of a Flash Sale at "historic" sale prices is the best form of marketing the company can do with so much inventory available.

When Nike was experiencing inventory problems and a decrease in margins another thing overlooked was that the margin results were actually a reflection of Nike's expenditures on opening new retail and warehousing facilities. Nike built a second gigantic distribution center in Memphis. Memphis now has 5 different Nike facilities. In 2014 Nike had 858 retail stores (in different divisions and brands: Hurley, Converse, etc.). In 2016 Nike had increased to more than 931 retail stores. This number continues to grow. Nike also did something I stated most brands had to consider, they opened smaller stores. Nike opened brand stores within JC Penny, and recently they launched an experimental boutique in Los Angeles that has inventory guided by data found within their Nike Apps for the region. The experimental store should be a major red flag to Nike retail accounts. If Nike makes a decision to encroach on the Sneaker Boutique format this could be a major issue especially since part of the CDO was to create personalized training for those within the App. The small retail store in Los Angeles was also hosting workout classes. In 2016 Nike filed a patent for an adjustable Fitness Area. In 2018 Nike opened a small location based on data from their App with a small fitness area for training and trying on footwear and apparel. Their recent Jumpman LA location[16], for Jordan Brand, improved on the personalized aspect. Jumpman LA actually incorporates a training facility with a full length basketball court. A customer has the ability to try on gear and as Nike decides to utilize personal trainers as a part of the customer service experience why would an athlete visit any other store for gear? This is a bit of an aside. As local municipalities are being closed by city governments unable to afford the cost associated with running community centers, I see in Nike an opportunity to further assimilate into neighborhoods via sports programs for its most dedicated customer.

If I use Memphis as a reference, Nike's new multimillion dollar distribution facility is located in one of the toughest neighborhoods in the city. Inside of the Nike Employee Store they host

[16] https://arch-usa.com/jumpman-la-is-the-next-stage-of-nikes-80-20-strategy/

workouts that are open to visitors. Foot Locker, City Gear and Hibbett Sports in Memphis are in the tenuous position of competing against Nike on three fronts creating what I think is one of the most difficult retail districts in the country. It's a situation that I envision happening everywhere in a much more concise and efficient manner.

Apple has small stores built around the tactile customer experience. Nike is preparing to launch a yoga line for men. The natural progression is for Nike to open yoga studios. If that is the case, then Jumpman LA is a predictor of Nike possibly shifting to training academies and sponsored gyms. This summation of what is happening with Nike's CDO only scratches the surface.

Chapter 7

Nike's Consumer Direct Offense and Amazon

Without Point Of Sales[17] data for retailers there can only be a hypothetical analysis made about how Nike's shift has already affected the stores Nike has wholesale accounts with. A more concrete analysis can arrive from a data set generated from a long term retail experiment. I took the time in 2018 to perform that experiment. This section won't dive into those statistics, but making any statement about Nike's CDO creates an opportunity for a rebuttal of *post hoc ergo propter hoc*. In other words this book and every page can be disregarded without a complete data set showing that Nike's CDO and their ability to reach their consumer at a higher rate than their wholesale accounts is a problem. It isn't a logical fallacy to see Nike

[17] When you visit a store and make a purchase your information is captured by the company and can be used to inform future decisions by the company.

offering discounted items at wholesale prices on their footwear and apparel while their retailers are attempting to fight the fact that at any point Nike could literally wipe out their wholesale accounts' margins by creating a race based on reduced prices.

Nike's wholesale accounts are encountering a machine in Nike that is slowly chipping away at one of the few areas of growth remaining for brick and mortar store chains, e-commerce. During Investor's Day Nike explained in great detail how much growth they are looking at via digital. During my transcription of the event I added my own comments in parenthesis:

Nike Direct Discussion

2.8 Billion visits at 7000 doors.

In depth discussion on **Nikeplus Membership** (memberships have grown 30% at 100 million people) Nikeplus looks to grow by 3x members. Nike Direct will have member only products. (Hmmm concept of exclusivity)

Changing the merchandising (a third of products will be exclusive to NDC). Freshness Through Express Lane Next 5 years 50% of seasonal products will be available via Express Lane. Member First will be personalized via algorithms and machine learning for personalized experience.

5 Platforms

Nike App, SNKRS, Nike Run Club, NDC, Nike Training Club (All Apps are omnichannel connecting through all 5 apps and to retail)

There is a reason Nike has been so effective at reaching their customer. "Nike Inc.'s market share is poised to expand, as both its processing and delivery times are faster than competitors." This quote is from an article written in 2016[18]; long before there was a name for Nike's Consumer Direct Offense. For years I explained that Nike's growth was heavily shaped by the company being located in Memphis. The *Financial Post* article for the above quote confirmed my hypothesis with one simple form of support; an article on distribution.

When this article was written analysts and business websites had been stating that Nike was losing ground in the sneaker wars. I had been stating that Nike wasn't losing ground in the sneaker battle. My discussion centered on the fact that shoe stores, online and brick and mortar, were closing as a direct result of Nike's decision to

[18] https://arch-usa.com/insider-ties-nike-keeps-winning-financial-post/

provide more revenue for their shareholders by building their DTC market.

In order for Nike to build DTC the distribution had to be in place. It's like *Frank Lucas* trying to sell *Blue Magic* without *cor-nerboys*… you just *can't* do it. For Nike this meant that being in Memphis was critical to their growth after their big slump in the 80s.

The Financial Post article gave a breakdown of why Nike out-performs its counterparts. What isn't mentioned is the fact that Memphis is home to Swoosh distribution; not Portland or China, Memphis. Memphis is also home to Fed Ex's shipping hub. You know who handles smart post by USPS? Fed Ex. You know what city controls shipping for UPS in the south? Memphis. In other words the speed in which Nike can get your packages to you enhances its DTC and in turn creates a company that can outperform its competitors.

Under Armour and adidas don't have distribution hubs in this region? You know who does? Asics. Asics, has a warehouse just south of Memphis in Byhalia, Mississippi. Even New Balance has opened a distribution facility just above Memphis in St. Louis. These new warehouses for smaller brands hints at one important factor, brands are becoming very aware of direct-to-consumer and they are establishing the distribution strategy to increase sales via their own doors.

Nike during Investor's Day discussed taking their 30,000 wholesale partners down to 40. As Nike removes wholesale channels they will begin to enforce MSRP and advertising requirements for those partners. Retail locations relying heavily on promo will not be able to highlight their price options on closeout items. This could lead to Nike reps visiting locations often to ensure policies are being enforced. With expenses for retailers rising with the redesign of stores (a requirement to retain a Nike account), training employees, and infrastructure, margins will be eroded. One of the few opportunities for growth for companies in Nike's wholesale chains is e-commerce, but smaller urban accounts are relying on a moat that is no longer a large chasm, cash customers.

My earlier discussions on the multiple digital retail outlets and the information I wrote above about Nike's digital strategy is where the biggest issues for stores like City Gear, EbLens, Jimmy Jazz, DTLR, Shoe Palace and Villa will occur. Brick and Mortar locations benefit from the percentage of cash customers who still visit stores. As many smaller chains operate in urban markets this is a place of security for the chains. However, it should be noted that the *Un-banked*[19] population that has been the backbone of urban accounts, is slowly becoming *Banked* in a different way. Cash customers are utilizing options such as PayPal.me and Cash App which both have credit card options for these users. These traditionally unbanked customers are now capable of experiencing online retail for the first time.

As a point of reference Amazon, where many third party sellers in footwear are, is a company that has recognized that continued growth means finding a way to acquire shoppers who aren't online. Amazon is working with many brands to open registries[20].

---

[19] Unbanked customers are typically low-income people who don't utilize banks to keep their money. This sector of people use payday loans and check cashing options to pay bills and therefore aren't a part of the digital eco-system.

[20] Brand registry is a program where a brand can open a store on Amazon. This allows brands to control pricing on the largest e-commerce platform in the world.

These registries provide Amazon with inventory the site hasn't had in a consistent and readily available manner. Because Amazon is not a shoe manufacturer (this is changing with private labels) the site had to rely primarily on third party sellers to attract sneaker enthusiasts. Those sneakerheads consist of large numbers of the unbanked. Retail outlets, small and big chains, not only have to account for Nike's continued push into their margins; they also have to pay attention to Amazon, as well as all of the third party digital outlets mentioned earlier. How is Amazon going after the unbanked? Amazon Cash[21]:

> Amazon Cash allows people to visit a number of locations to pay cash for items on Amazon. Here are a couple of locations of where people can pay cash:
>
> 7/11, Boost Mobile, CVS Pharmacy, Game Stop[22]

PayPal.me, Cash App, and Amazon Cash are challenges that are not really being discussed by chains as a reason for concern. Amazon Cash is going to be bolstered by Amazon's Last Mile delivery program and the build out of Amazon Fulfillment centers in strategic

[21] https://arch-usa.com/how-amazon-plans-to-reach-those-who-use-cash-to-buy-kicks-amazon-cash/

[22] https://arch-usa.com/how-amazon-plans-to-reach-those-who-use-cash-to-buy-kicks-amazon-cash/

areas throughout the country. As Amazon's Last Mile program is implemented they will find a way to cater to the customers in areas where delivery could be a problem. Nike is already finding a way in the international market.

Nike's CDO is not being discussed in many circles for retail. This is a mistake and should be at the forefront of every discussion by all footwear chains. The fact that unbanked people are now actively learning to participate in the online market is what has empowered sites like StockX and GOAT. During any retail dive you can overhear customers who would probably have never considered buying from Nike.com less than a year ago, use their smart phones in store to comparison shop. As Nike refines programs within their CDO they are also implementing programs internationally that will without a doubt arrive in the U.S. for urban markets.

One of the primary reasons retailers did not have to worry about losing cash customers to digital was cash customers tend to live in areas where package delivery is not really an option. In Japan last year Nike created a "bodega" based shipping system. It is a system that Amazon is working on as well and already utilizing in their

Whole Foods stores. Nike's system is called Konbini[23]. "Nike is using the local bodega, corner grocery, or Konbini in Japan to make sure orders are placed in a routine path for the customers to get their packages on the way home. While public transit in Japan is much better than it is in most US cities, the Konbini delivery system, "… brings the best of Nike to the epicenter of consumers' daily lives in Japan, meeting consumers where they are – at the konbini – whether that's on the main floor of their apartment building, next door to their children's school, within the train station, or around the corner from a local hotel. The delivery locations will be located in almost every neighborhood across the country."

Note the locations listed in regard to Nike's Konbini program: Children's School, Train Station, Local Hotel. It takes a lot of foresight to make projections, but when you consider that low-income people utilize their smart phones for internet access and that the mobile device has become a considerable tool in shopping, it is not a stretch to realize that the consumers visiting local footwear and apparel stores are going to be integrated into the digital shopping

---

[23] https://arch-usa.com/can-nike-com-japans-new-delivery-service-catch-on-in-the-united-states/

environment. If these cash based businesses don't prepare for this via an omnichannel experience for their cash customers I believe within a year the digital disruption will begin to affect the smaller chains.

While this discussion is obviously based on e-commerce and many of the moves Nike is making like implementing "konbini" in the U.S. will not be implemented until a few years from now, it is imperative that smaller chains begin to understand what is ahead for them in relation to Nike. Nike is going to dominate the majority of their distribution. They will work in conjunction with the large wholesale accounts like Foot Locker and the recently acquired by JD Sports -Finish Line to ensure that they still have product available in traditional settings of course, but even large retailers should be aware that there is a fine line when working with a brand that has become emboldened by their digital strategy. Foot Locker is in a better position due to the sheer size of the company and that can be seen in programs Nike discussed during their Investor's Day.

Nike has made the decision to align with Footlocker via Nike trained "athletes" (sales leads), working in Footlocker stores in key cities. Many new footwear releases, which have been traditionally the primary drivers of foot traffic to brick and mortar, are already being launched via SNKRS App and Nike.com. Nike is also releasing Quickstrike[24] footwear with Footlocker only. Unless there are specially planned products only launching via smaller retail chains, releases relegated to Nike and Footlocker will cut into traffic in store and online for the small chains. Nike is also working out the details allowing them to sell products via Instagram. The cash customer is on IG and their engagement there expedites their integration into the digital ecosystem.

Nike established an Instagram trial in London. If Nike continues to merchandise social and they add to their 7000 doors, the only natural outcome for chains is that they will feel the pinch. Small retailers have to begin planning to fight against this. How does that happen when Nike has unlimited capital to experiment and implement new strategies? Stores like KicksUSA are probably like many chains in that cash is often tied into inventory and payroll leaving very little opportunity to push money into acquiring customers in the digital area. This is the problem. What is the solution?

---

[24] High demand footwear and products released by Nike in limited quantities in limited locations.

That is a rhetorical question. I wanted to establish the Nike effect before delivering more information that moves this discussion from CDO's influence on retail to CDO's creation of one of the most effective platforms in third party; a platform that I took a close look at over the course of one year: StockX. I can't move into a discussion on StockX without delivering a discussion on why I think the pureplay e-commerce channel could be one of the best online platforms in the world. Now there is an irony in discussing StockX as one of the best third party resale platforms.

Amazon is the largest, fastest growing retailer in the world. Up until a few years ago Amazon did not really 'own' any inventory. When you think about a company like Lyft and Uber or Air BnB, these are companies founded on Amazon's principle of 'no ownership'. Amazon built a delivery system. At any time Sears, Toys-R-Us, or The Sports Authority (all now bankrupt) could have invested heavily in a digital strategy to offset Amazon's platform. Kind of like Blockbuster could have invested in streaming, but Netflix came along and wiped out a long standing business.

Amazon created a delivery system that allowed third party and brands to warehouse their goods and forget about it: Amazon Fulfillment. The program Fulfillment by Amazon (FBA) allows businesses to ship their products to an Amazon warehouse and *let the sales roll in*. There is a problem with using FBA. The brands and third party sellers using FBA give all of their customers to Amazon and Amazon takes care of the dirty work of shipping and handling returns. This has been a great thing for many small businesses. I personally benefitted from working through Amazon for years, until I realized what I did to myself. Brands selling through Amazon have incredible access to the powerful Prime platform. That access comes at the price of building a stronger business. Amazon knows this and Nike is showing that they know this as well.

Chapter 8

Amazon: The Biggest 3rd Party Platform

So far the discussion in this book has been about Nike's CDO and the introduction to third party and why retail should be discussing these two things continuously. In order for this book to make sense I have to make things a bit more personal. As I stated earlier I don't have POS data for the industry. What I do have is my own data which I've used as a micro to macro comparison that has allowed me to correctly predict the acquisition of City Gear and the resurgent stock value of Nike as well as the recent downward trend of adidas. I don't make claims lightly. I take the time to analyze and research and deliver facts that become the foundation of ideas.

I brought up *Fulfillment by Amazon* but I didn't mention the *Seller's Marketplace on Amazon*[25]. These Amazon programs provide sellers with a fantastic reach. The seller doesn't have to keep a database or send e-mails constantly. The seller doesn't have to market unless they want to, and the seller is given access to a marketplace where the consumer keeps their information on file and can make a purchase with one click, or no clicks with voice ordering via Alexa. Amazon is a behemoth that allows you to slowly fall asleep and die without pain. Did you catch that? Go back and read that sentence again.

Amazon is euthanasia for small business and brands. Amazon doesn't set out to kill a company. A seller/brand makes a decision to end it all the moment they sign up with Amazon. While there are probably arguments against what I'm saying here I experienced firsthand Amazon's transition from a company that supported its third party to a company entering the third party marketplace. As Amazon entered third party as a seller, they systematically wiped out smaller

[25] Seller's Marketplace on Amazon allows third party sellers to create a store on Amazon and sell goods.

third party sellers which created the unintentional effect of allowing StockX, GOAT and other third party platforms to rise.

The third party sales in the sneaker business began on the message boards of Niketalk and found a home originally via eBay. Since 2009 Amazon and eBay have battled for the sellers carrying kicks. eBay was the best platform, but Amazon's acquisition of Zappos opened the door to footwear sales on Amazon, which led to sellers leaving eBay for the Amazon Marketplace. Amazon is the standard in e-commerce, so it is easier to build this discussion by starting with Amazon. Below is data from a post I wrote about the resale market[26]. The post was in regard to a prominent sneaker analyst's opinion on the value and size of the resale market. The analyst posited that the influence of resale was minimal based on numbers on the Campless website (now StockX). The numbers were not accurate because they failed to include Amazon:

> "Total sales of sport footwear in the US last year were $22 billion. This makes the sneakerhead portion about 5% of the total US business." By only analyzing eBay and Campless' data this 5% number is possibly

[26] https://arch-usa.com/npds-matt-powell-wrong-sneakerheads/

incorrect. Here are a few facts about the third party marketplace on Amazon:

"The Seattle company said Monday third-party merchants were responsible for 2 billion items sold last year, double the total in 2013, even as the number of such businesses held about steady compared with the prior period at "more than 2 million…Those merchants sold more than 40 percent of the items Amazon unloaded last year, according to a statement, suggesting a total of at least 5 billion items sold."

L2 states that Amazon controls over 50% of online transactions. There isn't any way to breakdown how much of this is in sneakers. The *5 billion items sold* information, from 2014, is in regard to all items on Amazon and there isn't any way to narrow down the exact number of shoes sold on Amazon, but when you consider the retail/resale market also includes Zappos which was acquired by Amazon for 1.2 Billion another story begins to take shape. Since there isn't any way to pull data from Amazon, I have to make the study smaller. If we look at my shop on Amazon as a microcosm of the sellers there we can get a better grasp of the comparison to eBay and Campless' data.

This is a list of the top sneaker resellers on eBay via Campless[27]. In the article, an analyst used the information there to estimate the resale market: the top two sellers made 2.7 Million, and 1.7 Million respectively. The third place seller in this year earned only 300,000 dollars. My store on Amazon is one of the smallest stores. As I said I don't have a count of how many third party shoe sellers are on the platform, but I very rarely won the buybox. From 2011 to 2016 I had to constantly adjust prices against a number of older

[27] https://stockx.com/sneaker-blog/top-25-ebay-sellers-and-131k-more

sellers. In 2014 Amazon began adjusting their guidelines for selling footwear and an influx of counterfeit sellers and sellers from other channels were able to begin selling. While there were hundreds of sellers on certain shoes, on older more obscure footwear there were still at least 20 other stores listed.

I can't triangulate, but if the data from Campless has 1300 sellers from eBay, Amazon has possibly two times as many sellers with revenues that are much higher. How can I say this? From 2012 to 2013 the ARCH Online Shop, one of the smallest on Amazon earned almost 1 Million dollars. If the ARCH Online Shop had been included in Josh Luber's Campless data from 2014, I would have been the third place seller on the list with around $350,000 in sales:

From December 2012 to December 2014 I had over 600,000 dollars in sales. This speaks towards how much money both big and small retail leaves on the table in digital sales. Third party marketplace sellers don't typically have wholesale accounts with brands. The inventory I use in sales comes from chains that have discounted older product or released product that held a higher value due to interest/hype.

In math we can do a ratio to make an estimate. If my one man shop would have been included on this list, then the biggest shops on Amazon possibly earned 3 times as much as the top two shops on eBay. This is all guess work, but here is a statistic about Amazon's growth in comparison to eBay based on an article from Bloomberg[28]:

[28] https://www.bloomberg.com/news/articles/2015-04-06/amazon-woos-ebay-s-once-loyal-merchants-with-faster-sales-growth

EBay Inc.'s once-loyal merchants are moving more of their business to Amazon.com Inc., saying they get more for their money by selling merchandise via the Web retailer. Amazon's pool of merchants climbed to more than 2 million in 2014, while the number of sellers on EBay has remained flat at about 25 million in the past two years. Businesses that at first set up online storefronts on EBay say they're surprised how quickly sales surge on Amazon once products appear on both sites.

Chris Matsakis, president of daily-deal site DealGenius.com in Chicago, said that as recently as 2013 sales on EBay exceeded those on Amazon's marketplace. Last year, his revenue via Amazon grew fivefold, and are now four times greater than sales on EBay, he said.

"We're seeing significant growth on Amazon where EBay has sort of plateaued," Matsakis said.

I know a comparison of different products being sold is not a way to make a comparison, but all I'm doing is offering an opposing theory. If we can consider that Chris Matsakis' growth was 5 times, and we apply that to the 5% number of the value of resale based on eBay data, the number could possibly change dramatically when we analyze resale including Amazon.

I think the error in estimates derives from the fact that Campless only assigns value to Jordan Brand or "hyped" shoes. Even on their own platform StockX, they are missing a considerable part of the market because there isn't any way for the site to sell to the average customer. Cheap shoes aren't listed at all, only hyped *reseller* shoes, but sneakerheads buy "beaters"[29] also. If you consider my shop as a microcosm, I very rarely sell Retros, but I'm an avid sneaker fan and so are countless other third party sellers on Amazon.

Update:

I was asked what my estimate of the resale market is so I wrote some e-mails and did some more research.

According to IBISworld, online sales of footwear between Amazon and Footlocker is 12 Billion.

L2 states that Amazon controls over 50% of all online sales. While the 12 Billion appears to be split 50/50 I'm making a guess that Amazon controls about 60% of this market based on third party and Zappos and a better sales machine. This means that Amazon is possibly taking in 7.2 Billion in footwear. Since the sales on IBISworld list Amazon against Footlocker, I can reasonably assume that this is athletic footwear being analyzed.

According to the articles above 3rd party sellers are right at 50% on Amazon. This means that 3.6 billion of sales could be 3rd party sellers.

If Amazon has around 3 Billion in resale, added to the 1.1 Billion from eBay, the resale market is no longer at 5%, it could be between 15-20%.

[29] Beaters are shoes that aren't considered important in the sneaker culture. They are daily wear kicks that may be damaged and used for performance or other things outside of style. There isn't any resale value in a pair of beaters.

This long quote is to establish that resale and third party marketplaces are a true threat to the growth of brick and mortar retail online shops. Since I wrote the information above StockX has changed. I stated in the long quote that StockX is for *hype* shoe releases. Over the course of 2018, as I've stated, I sold there and the data shows that the platform is actually becoming a base for shoes that are general releases which can be found in retail stores on a daily basis. It is no longer just a platform for high end releases which is why StockX is more of a disruption than retailers understand. This moves the discussion too far ahead. Let's go back to my time on eBay and Amazon.

For the record I was a 5 star seller on both platforms. I left eBay in 2011 and was accepted into Amazon Marketplace for footwear in October of 2011. In the discussion on footwear sales what is often overlooked is that almost half of Amazon's inventory is sourced from third party sellers on the Amazon Marketplace. According to Seeking Alpha, "Over 47% of units that are shipped are actually sold by a third-party seller on Amazon."

In my best year on Amazon and as a third party seller I generated $718,678 dollars gross. From 2011 to 2016 I generated over 3 million dollars gross. Amazon, since 2015, began building a wall around the sneaker third party marketplace. That wall is why I've stated that any person or business selling on Amazon is performing digital euthanasia. Let me explain.

When Amazon acquired Zappos in 2009 they did so because they did not have the technology and business plan to sell shoes efficiently. After acquiring Zappos, the third party on Amazon began to grow encroaching upon eBay. Footlocker had begun building out their e-commerce at the same time and saw considerable growth there, but Amazon had access to a multi-million dollar company and they utilized Zappos to learn footwear. By 2015 Amazon began building direct relationships with sneaker brands through their brand registry program. Zappos' presence on Amazon.com was reduced.

I became aware of Amazon Brand Registry when I launched my footwear company ARCH. To be admitted into the brand registry I had to register with the GS1 to own my barcodes which enabled me to sell my footwear on Amazon's platform. From 2011 to 2014 I learned the *ins and outs* of how Amazon Brand Registry worked in conjunction with Amazon Ads to reach the consumer with a brand they had never heard of before. From 2012 to 2015 I sold over 600 pair of shoes that I had designed, had manufactured, and packaged and shipped.

I was able to run my shoe company brand because of the sales I attained as a third party sneaker shop. My e-commerce via Amazon was incredible from 2011 to 2014, but that began to change. One quick note, My 6 years on Amazon I was one of the only stores to maintain perfect feedback with over 600 customer reviews. In 2015, Amazon began forcing marketplace stores to adhere to Amazon's policies. At the same time my Amazon marketplace and all sellers were being affected by brand registry[30] and the influx of Chinese sellers on the Amazon platform[31]. Initially, Amazon's brand registry prevented everyone without an account from selling New Balance. The registry then added Coach and ASICS as styles requiring approval *from the*

---

[30] https://arch-usa.com/brand-gating-will-hit-sneaker-resale-big-way-holiday-season/

[31] https://arch-usa.com/insider-ties-amazon-is-full-of-chinese-counterfeits-and-theyre-driving-out-legit-goods/

brands to sell on Amazon Marketplace. Vans and Saucony have been added to the brand registry as well.

In 2016 I saw the shift in policies on Amazon and began adjusting my business. Amazon's brand registries gave them a direct relationship with footwear companies. They already had years of data from third party sellers to inform brands on what styles sold well via the platform. Amazon began utilizing the data to warehouse certain shoes. Many sneaker options that third party sellers like me were listing began to show up as *Fulfilled by Amazon*. The company used their brand registry to sell adidas *for* adidas. This gave adidas more control over the SRP on Amazon and it cut me and other sellers out on popular models.

I bought over 100 pair of an adidas NMD *all white* that was placed behind a **Brand Gate**[32]. There were two reasons this particular model was Brand Gated. Another Amazon seller sold an item a buyer said was *fake*. Amazon didn't distinguish between sellers who had

[32] A brand has the right to dictate where their product is sold. A brand gate allows the brand on Amazon to say what can and can't be sold. If a seller doesn't have an account that allows them to sell that brand on Amazon then that seller will be blocked from selling that item. All items aren't covered under the brand. It's usually the most popular item. This prevents counterfeits from entering the market as well.

great feedback or new sellers without feedback. They simply blocked everyone without an adidas contract from selling. To gain permission to sell the shoes again the seller had to submit proof from adidas that the item was sold to them by adidas. Since I purchased my shoes from authorized retail outlets I sent the receipts as evidence. Amazon didn't accept the receipts.

adidas under the Brand Registry began isolating footwear that was popular for them. Once adidas moved the all-white NMD behind the brand gate, third party sellers could no longer sell the shoe. This left me with over 60 pair of that model in inventory. (In a later chapter I will explain how 'brand registry' could undercut the entire third party marketplace and why the investment into consignment and third party platforms is a bit flawed.)

Amazon began diminishing the role of Zappos on the Amazon site around 2016. Amazon had added Under Armour, Saucony, adidas, and in 2017 they announced that Nike would be adding a brand registry. I initially saw Nike's addition as a major issue for third party and for traditional retail. Nike quickly released information explaining that the Amazon registry was more of a pilot program. Nike's registry did however immediately place popular models like the Air Jordan 11 Retro behind brand gates. Amazon has placed continued pressure on the marketplace sellers by forcing third party sellers to adhere to Amazon's selling and return policies. While this appears to be a boon for traditional retail since Amazon is diminishing the ability for third party to thrive, it is not. The consistent issues with returns, chargebacks, and claims on eBay, and Amazon led to the rise of sneaker e-commerce platforms as a disruption.

Sellers originally began *jumping ship* from eBay to Amazon in 2010. Around 2016 many sellers began to move back towards eBay because of Amazon's Brand Gating. There were some resellers who were earning considerable revenue on both eBay and Amazon marketplaces that were smart enough to transition to their own platforms. Those businesses began garnering investments and growing at a rapid rate.

Venture capital investments into apps and websites for resale took off around 2016. GOAT and StockX entered. I tested StockX during 2017 and made 14,000 dollars. This year I increased my research and decided to work exclusively through StockX while also continuing the adjustment to my business plan from 2015-16. In 2018 I sold enough footwear to create the data this book is based on. In the upcoming chapters I will share those totals and what will become clear is that the sales I had in 2018 are an indication of what small retail chains are up against with the third party marketplaces like Stadium Goods, Stash, Slang, HBX, Kixify, Flight Club, and GOAT. The sales total I had by the end of 2018 is also an indication of the failure of athletic footwear and apparel retailers to create a more integrated online/offline shopping experience. Stores rely on promotion as opposed to investment into their own marketing outlets. When you consider Foot Locker at one point had one of the best CMS/blogging platforms and release information sites in their *Foot Locker Unlocked* and the fact that the site hasn't been updated consistently, while websites like SoleCollector and Hypebeast remain so active in the creation of content they are now worth millions in ad revenue, it's evident that there is a disconnect even for the most dominant sneaker retailer in the industry.

As the third party businesses continue to grow in digital they are also beginning to look at brick and mortar. Once again, I will develop this discussion later in the book, but it has to be stated that both small and big retailers in athletic footwear and apparel are leaving considerable real estate on the table.

Think of this chapter as a board game of Monopoly. The players in the game are Nike CDO, Foot Locker, Smaller Retail Outlets and Third Party. Nike controls the Railroads, Boardwalk and Park Place. Foot Locker controls Water Works along with the Green, Yellow and Red real estate. Smaller Retail outlets like Hibbett Sports and Finish Line control the Electric Company and the Orange and Lavender area with St. Charles. Smaller Retail owns the Baltic and Vermont side of the board. Third Party Resell is, in all honesty, using the *Free Parking* so they can *Just Visit* in hopes that they don't *Go to Jail.*

Chapter 9

Amazon, Cash Customers & Private Label

Amazon hasn't worked *in conjunction* with Nike's CDO to create sites like StockX and GOAT. Although I *lumped* Amazon into *Third Party* in my Monopoly description, the company that is moving quickly towards a one trillion dollar value understands how tenuous their relationship is with brands. I have to explain why I placed a trillion dollar company into the Third Party tier on the least profitable side of the Monopoly board. While brands are creating registries, Amazon, like all third party platforms, maintains ZERO ownership of the brands they carry. If Nike continues to pull buyers into their digital sales apps and websites and other brands do the same, the natural progression is that sales will diminish for other companies. Right now it seems the brands are only beginning to realize the mistake they've made by creating brand registries with Amazon. Nike after over a year on Amazon still states clearly that their work with Amazon is increasing, but is in a pilot/testing phase. I believe the brand understands that it has to be a part of Amazon to maintain control of the presentation of their product on the platform, but if this is the case why would I say working with Amazon is a problem?

If anyone looks at the surface of adidas, Under Armour and Nike's brand registries what they will find is a series of companies going to where the customer is shopping. It's an easy and convenient way to reach customers and sell old inventory or launch exclusive inventory. Isn't this a positive on the surface? Brands have a presence on the largest e-commerce site in the world.

A deeper dive into why Amazon brand registry holds the key to disruption for brands and retail outlets lies in private labels. Let me move this to brick and mortar stores for a moment. Traditional retail has a play of its own in private label. As of right now only Foot Locker understands this and is making moves to secure their future as a company that isn't reliant solely on the success of Nike. I use Nike here because sneaker retail is beholden to Nike and their dominance at retail. As Nike continues pressing towards their *Apple Play*, other brands are following. Foot Locker is showing a blueprint for overcoming the inherent issues of competing directly with brands that are carried in store.

Foot Locker has been carrying private labels within their stores for a long time. Their private labels could offset the DTC push being made by Nike. Private label should be a strategy at regional stores like City Gear and DTLR. The regional chains tend to have more promotional offers available which drives foot traffic, but ultimately diminishes margins. Let me stick with Foot Locker. When Foot Locker has to rely on markdowns of Nike and adidas apparel it leaves the company at the mercy of regional stores. It also leaves the company at the mercy of the digital onslaught of e-mails and app notifications by brands delivering promotional materials to followers. The only place where Foot Locker Inc. really has an opening to protect itself from direct to consumer brand strategy is in the presentation of private label.

I visit local stores every day. During a visit to the local Footaction the manager and his sales lead were hard at work building displays and staging mannequins. I notice the apparel on every visit because it is located at the front of the store. On one particular day the footwear being presented in the front of the store was no longer adid-as or Nike, it was Vans. The apparel that was being merchandised was named Be.Spoke. I'm a fan of fashion and seeing the term *bespoke* hit me immediately. I took my phone out and began googling the brand. When I couldn't find any information I took a closer look at the items and realized that I'd seen a similar cut and style before at Champs with *CSG* which is the private label for Champs under Foot Locker Inc. The manager was doing such a good job of setting up the front of store that two guys who worked at a regional competitor walked in and looked at the gear immediately. One of them asked, "Y'all got Vans to match this?" The sales lead took over and walked him to the Vans section explaining that they just got a shipment in. The guy re-sponded, "I've been sending people to other stores cause we don't carry them." He paused and then added, "I like that set," pointing to the clothing being placed onto the mannequin.

The manager of the store was moving quickly around shifting entire racks of jackets and pants from the wall to the floor racks. The change of seasons makes it important that the shorts and tees be highlighted, but because this is Memphis and a thunderstorm could hit at any time, the jackets still needed to be prominent. What I was most impressed by is the fact that Footaction understands what the brands seem to ignore often, merchandising. On my website I wrote about Tretorn and the lack of merchandising with the Andre 3000 line at a regional store. Which moves me into discussing influencer marketing and I don't want to deviate; but I will say this, Tretorn worked with one of the most influential emcees in Hip-Hop to create a collection and the entire project fell flat. Not because Andre 3000 isn't dope, but because no one walking into the store knew that the Tretorn collection was by Andre 3000, not even the store manager and her assistant. That wasn't at Footaction so let me get back on track.

The reason I bring up the Tretorn collaboration was because the in store display of footwear and apparel hasn't changed in 30 years. The only place merchandising taking place is in the store window. Again, that's another topic… back to Be.Spoke

Footaction had a poster hanging at the front of the store. The person was styled in Be.Spoke apparel and wearing Vans. In 2018 Vans rocketed in popularity. The poster featured a model who looked a lot like 21 Savage wearing their Footaction private label apparel and a pair of Vans. I asked the store manager if the product was selling and he said that it was "alright" but he wished the company had consulted him.

Foot Locker obviously understands the importance of private labels and this was a very good move by the company, but it would behoove the people who are running the division to begin reaching out to store managers for more input. As a matter of fact before any real decision is made about the gear being produced, Foot Locker should build a committee of 50 store managers and form a workshop that allows the gear and upcoming releases to be selected by the store leaders. The reason I say this is because the use of the name Be.Spoke is a failure. The market that the clothes are being designed for isn't bespoke and probably doesn't have any idea of what bespoke means. The gear and name has to actually work together to make a cohesive product. Bespoke products are made to order. They are custom. Unless Foot Locker plans on offering a print on demand product or custom fit experience for their shoppers this name doesn't work and by default this could make it difficult to sell. Take Be.Spoke off as the label and replace it with Op.Tion and you have a script ready made for the sales leads to present to customers. I'm not saying that's a great name, but when you are moving a customer towards an unknown property it has to be made more familiar, or it better match up with a pair of the dopest shoes coming out.

I like the work being done by Foot Locker (Footaction). There is real opportunity there that compliments the upcoming release of the PENSOLE[33] shoe competition winner and gives Foot Locker an "option" to potentially launch its own "bespoke" footwear line for its

[33] PENSOLE was founded by D'Wayne Edwards and is a comprehensive "college" of study for prospective footwear designers. The academy is working with Foot Locker to launch footwear by students who compete in an annual footwear design competition.

apparel. Interestingly enough Foot Locker has not only made a decision to collaborate with PENSOLE, the company continues to invest into private label.

Stay with me, I know I began with a discussion on Amazon, but I'm building a case here to clarify why third party platforms are becoming one of the most important sectors in business although these platforms originally lacked any real ownership outside of contracts with brands.

Foot Locker at the start of 2019 invested in a small startup footwear company named Super Heroic[34]. I discussed this investment on the site:

> Super Heroic is taking an initiative based approach to creating a footwear company. The brand is building an interactive lifestyle for kids and shoes happen to be the delivery system. Jason Mayden is building an active lifestyle company. The shoes are the

[34] Super Heroic is a small footwear company utilizing footwear as the delivery system for improving the health of children through play. https://arch-usa.com/why-foot-lockers-investment-in-super-heroic-is-a-blueprint-move/

delivery system, but the goal is to make sure kids are getting off of the computer and the couch to participate in activities. An investment by Foot Locker is an investment into what is essentially a multifaceted sneaker community being developed where the company can offer the products that are utilized in this community. Why is this important?

While Foot Locker seems linked to Nike, they have been able to avoid slides by any brand that isn't performing well. When Nike was down a few years ago, Foot Locker adjusted by allowing adidas to lead the wall. Foot Locker also adjusted when adidas was no longer selling by placing retro lifestyle brands like Vans and Fila at the front of their stores. Their ability to move in line *with and around* the brands they carry is critical to their shareholders. What is even more critical is that as every brand moves toward DTC it diminishes the power of retailers who don't have private labels to offset the inherent problems with battling the company that makes the product the retailer is selling.

Super Heroic is in its infancy, but they are catering to a segment where it isn't about disposable income. Kids need shoes more than anyone because of their growth patterns. Parents are also looking for activities for their kids and if they can gain information from Foot Locker on Super Heroic events this decreases marketing costs and builds community. Now, everything I'm saying depends on Foot Locker carrying the footwear which isn't the case just yet, but think about this:

An investment into Super Heroic gives Foot Locker a private label footwear company in one of the most important segments in footwear.

How exactly does my deviation into private label and Foot Locker support how I started this section? If Foot Locker is the largest retailer of sneakers in the world and they understand the importance of private label, Amazon, the largest marketplace in the world launching private label while also hosting brands and gathering data on the best-selling items for brands is a serious issue.

Amazon is the most dangerous disruption for both retailers and brands in athletic apparel because with Amazon Cash in play, Amazon's introduction of performance apparel under private labels could become an issue for urban retail as well:

> In L2's latest report they have shown that, "While Amazon's private brands have historically been most successful competing with low-priced basic merchandise, more recent contemporary offerings pose risk of greater competition for legacy name brands. Amazon's activewear brand Peak Velocity sells a $79 hoodie that has a Best Seller rank of #38 in the Active Hoodies category, one of Nike's strongest categories."
>
> Amazon initially refrained from telling customers that the brands were Amazon brands. They are now proudly displaying that you are purchasing "OUR BRAND".

> Here is what is most compelling…Peak didn't exist prior to October 31st of 2017. Peak in less than a month is now ranked 38th in hoodies.[35]

Small retailers typically carry more urban apparel. However, the fact that Amazon is beginning to utilize Amazon Cash and *Unbanked* customers are learning to navigate the online shopping market, all retailers should be paying attention to Amazon private label and Amazon brand registry as a potential disruption. This is something that should be considered by all athletic footwear and apparel companies as well.

---

[35] https://arch-usa.com/l2-just-updated-their-report-on-amazon-private-labels-will-nike-ua-and-adidas-pay-attention-now/

Chapter 10

Why Does Resale Exist?

When I discussed brand gating as it related to my Amazon Marketplace experience I didn't explain in greater detail why that was important. In many ways the purpose of this book could wipe out how I continue to make money, but it won't. This book is one of experience… and research, but primarily it's an experienced based book that opens the door to a very serious question. If athletic footwear and apparel retailers were doing what they are supposed to be doing, would *third party resale only* exist? Maybe, but I say no. Third party resale would still exist, but only as a vehicle for wholesale account holders to liquidate old product. Is that clear?

Third party marketplaces only have a few paths to generate revenue:

1. Footwear has to be extremely limited by the brand and it has to inspire a desire to have the product. Take a moment to look up Jeff Staple and Nike Dunk. The shoe created by the designer is considered the model that created the hype around sneaker releases and resale. The shoe was only dropped at Staple's store and the NYC police had to arrive on the scene to prevent a riot. When a shoe is limited and hyped it commands a resale value. This type of resale is not really generating enough money to raise concerns for retail outlets or for the brands. There are only so many shoes available and there are only so many people willing to pay 1000 plus dollars for pairs.
2. When a model is made readily available by a brand, but the shoe holds considerable importance to the sneaker world there can be opportunities for third party vendors to capitalize by buying pairs to sell. Take for instance the Air Jordan 11 Retro Concord that released in December 2018.

Nike made over a million pair. The shoe retails at 220.00. Seven years ago a similar model released in similar numbers, but this was prior to the rise of Grailed, GOAT, and StockX. The only places resale was really taking place was on Amazon and eBay. This limited amount of marketplaces and the fact that although supply was plentiful, there were still people who couldn't get the shoe, meant that the 2012 Air Jordan 11 release was a shoe that could be resold for 350.00 dollars the day of release. There were a number of shoes like this released last year, but because the market has been shaped by third party the buyer now wins because the marketplace for resale is set by the buyer. I will explain this more later. Resale in this way only happens because some people don't want to deal with the lines or frustration of back door deals taking place with store managers selling models to guys dropping them off 25 to 100 dollars a pair. *Important* kicks will command a price above retail, just as *limited* release kicks resale.

3. The third place where resale is capable of happening is the one that is the foundation of this book. Hibbett Sports is a publicly traded company worth millions. They just launched an ecommerce platform less than two years ago. Eblens is a small retail chain in the Northeast. With over fifty stores it would seem that an online presence would already exists. Eblens doesn't have an online platform. I've mentioned City Gear several times in this book. They were just purchased by Hibbett Sports. Whether there are agreements in place with wholesale accounts that prevents the company from doing a better job of marketing and listing product for sale on their websites, I'm not sure. The fact is that City Gear has several outlets where they carry shoes that easily bring in profit for resellers. If City Gear had a better social media and website design they would capture the sales that third party sellers generate by buying shoes from the store and selling through the multitude of e-commerce platforms out there.

There is one really big issue that sits at the core of why retailers are failing at finding the customer who is buying on Amazon and eBay and that is retailers at brick and mortar are so focused on foot traffic into their locations that the online strategy consists of running an ad or shooting a picture and posting it to social media. There isn't a real strategy. It's a problem that I had myself when Amazon began forcing marketplace stores to adhere to Amazon policies. What I didn't do while I ran my Amazon shop is probably the most important section of this book. In this discussion there is a cautionary tale for any retailer out there. This isn't a sneaker related section. This is a business section. If there is person or a group launching a business this is where the sticky notes and red pen marks should cover the page. I'm about to climb into a problem and solution for retail.

Chapter 11

Amazon Was My Pimp

The entire time that I was making one million dollars every two years selling via Amazon, I had ignored my own platform. I didn't realize the mistake I made until 2015. I will get to that mistake, actually those mistakes, but first I want to look at a topic that I get questions about all of the time.

Those of you reading who have contacted me via YouTube or by e-mail to ask if you should open a sneaker shop this short section is for you. Those reading this who haven't asked me this question before and you're wondering what my answer is to, "Should I open a sneaker store?"My answer is always *no*. I then have to adjust my answer and state that if the person has a real system in place and they are very smart about how they operate the store they can open a sneaker shop. I usually don't go into more detail as my goal isn't to crush dreams, but to give information. What I haven't had a chance to do with anyone who asks about opening a store is to go into detail about my own business. That's what I'm doing here. I had a physical location that worked primarily as storage, but that created overhead.

The sneakerheads who are interested in diving into retail may not be aware of how a store runs. I recently saw a store in Arkansas open as a retail shop without an account; this means the store owner didn't get a shipment of shoes from a brand on a regular basis. Without an account the owner was building the business by buying discounted items from various stores. Inventory for the shop also arrived via consignment and they purchased footwear and apparel from different places. The owner started the business on eBay and then shifted to Amazon. Amazon gave the owner a false sense of confidence. I will talk in great detail about how Amazon gives sellers the perception that they are doing very good business by telling my own story.

Let's get back to the example of the sneaker shop owner in Arkansas. The owner grew quickly on Amazon before making the move to a brick and mortar. Does Amazon work and provide considerable revenue? Working with a team of two other guys on Amazon the sneaker shop owner in Arkansas generated enough money for the three man team because they didn't have a physical location. It didn't matter that they were reselling items bought from traditional retail, they could turn a profit. All of this changed as Amazon began to push brand registry and Amazon changed how independent seller run marketplaces operated. I can't say if I was one of the first shops to experience the problems associated with Amazon Seller Central Marketplace, but through my own research I'm one of the few to discuss the problems openly. I'm moving too far ahead. I'm writing about two different examples. I will finish the story of the Arkansas run *sneakerhead* store first.

When the team that opened the store in Arkansas saw the numbers from Amazon they pivoted to brick and mortar. This *in theory* was a good idea. The problem is once an e-commerce team opens a physical location a different set of problems arise. As Amazon's policies changed and the Arkansas sneaker shop encountered the problems with operating on razor thin margins, the owner had to reconsider keeping the store opened. Resale is not consistent in the margins generated and buying discounted items is a risk. There is a reason the products are discounted. In short, the Arkansas shop closed and the sellers shifted back to online only via another third party platform. This story example is for the benefit of the sneakerhead crowd.

The following example is for anyone who doesn't understand the costs associated with opening a shop. Let's consider that there is a small sneaker shop. The average annual gross revenue for the location is 500,000 dollars. This number is actually realistic for small sneaker retail shops. Let's break down the store income.

A store is a 500,000 dollar a year business. Sounds good doesn't it? The shop is paying 250,000 for the sneakers they are selling and they are making 250,000 dollars. (Realize that no one makes 100% profit. I'm creating a best case scenario, but not really.) The store owner pays a manager 60,000 dollars a year. Two assistant managers are earning 35,000 per year and 8 part time employees make

15,000 per year. That's a total of 250,000 dollars a year in expenditures. The store would be operating at break even. If the store owner is the manager and is earning a 60,000 salary, this would be great. The unfortunate part in this example is that the owner/manager has to pay the lease at 5000 per month. This means the store is operating at a negative 60,000 and even worse the chain is sitting on 50,000 dollars in inventory at the end of the year.

This store is going to go bankrupt or the store has to make a decision to cut hours or they have to find a way to make up the 110,000. Is it possible to make up this amount of money? How does this example tie into the first paragraph of this chapter where I said I would discuss my background? My Amazon Seller Central experience offers an insider's perspective on why third party platforms have been able to grow in the current sneaker retail environment. Amazon seemed like the perfect situation for me because I didn't have as much overhead as a retail store. Let's go back to the sneakerhead who transitioned from the eBay/Amazon store to a physical brick and mortar location. The seller who did this made the same huge mistake that I did. The seller saw Amazon as a savior. The reality is Amazon is a parasite. The only stores capable of utilizing the platform and surviving are brands big enough to offset the immediate loss of 15% to Amazon fees. Once again this gets me too far ahead.

The Arkansas sneaker store that opened a physical location completely ignored their website and utilized Amazon exclusively with some eBay tossed in. I made the same decision. When 2015 arrived Amazon changed the game for third party. Actually Nike changed the game. When I wrote that third party can only exist because of the things in the previous section, I should have wrote that brands can literally wipe out third party in one move, increased inventory. What happened to me as I've said was a cautionary tale that I shared, but no one was listening. I'm sharing it again.

In 2015 I began to experience serious issues with Amazon, but I ignored them and continued utilizing the platform to the detriment of my entire business model. Amazon does not allow you to connect with your customer. It is against policy to speak directly to the person you are selling to. Amazon does not want their marketplace vendors to direct buyers to the vendor's own site. eBay is the same. This was an issue that I overlooked for years because it seemed that I was making an incredible amount of money.

To bounce back to Nike's Consumer Direct Offense, the only reason it works is because Nike has all of their shoppers' contact information from the Apps or from the customers logging in to their websites. At any moment Nike can shoot an e-mail to every customer that has interacted with the platform. I could never do this on eBay or Amazon. If I bought 10,000 dollars in inventory I could put it on my Amazon shop and then I would have to hope for the best. I could not let my customers know I had a restock. If you want to kill a business this is the first step in doing so.

Let's get personal. Here are my 1099K[36] totals from Amazon solely. I was also wholesaling footwear at the time and that amount shows up on my taxes, but not on the 1099K from Amazon:

[36] 1099K - A payment settlement entity (PSE) must file Form 1099-K for payments made in settlement of reportable payment transactions for each calendar year. A PSE makes a payment in settlement of a reportable payment transaction, that is, any payment card or third party network transaction, if the PSE submits the instruction to transfer funds to the account of the participating payee to settle the reportable payment transaction. (IRS)

My first year on Amazon was 2011. I launched at the end of the year in November around Black Friday: **$41,469.59** I made 41,000 dollars in a month on Amazon. I quit teaching college the next semester. My income as a college professor was right at 40,000 teaching a full load of classes. I did make more as a high school teacher, but if I could make 41K in one month, I knew I could make a ton working full time through Amazon. When you take into consideration that I had always worked in education since I entered the sneaker business in 2004, I never worked full time as a reseller. I relied solely on my income and resell was used to pay for my first foray into making shoes with my Sho-Shot basketball shoes and basketball camps. I had never, at any point, earned my annual salary in 30 days. Sho-Shot was a strain financially and I bankrupted the business in 2007. In 2011 I had been consulting for a small school in Mississippi and teaching literature at the local community college. Launching the store on Amazon in November of 2011 and earning $41,000 dollars in a month… the feeling was intoxicating.

My second year on Amazon full time was 2012: **$450,712.63**

My third year on Amazon was 2013: **$456,372.17**

My fourth year on Amazon was 2014. My income total for 2014 was: **$297,544.69**. This year shows a considerable drop off. In a video interview with Tayib Salami, the other half of our ARCH x Housakicks Network, we had a discussion that's on YouTube. In 2014 Amazon did something that would begin the degradation of the platform for third party sellers. When I originally moved to Amazon it was a six month process. I had to redesign my website to adhere to Amazon guidelines. Amazon forced me to build a website that they approved of. The pictures on the site had to be completely white and at least 1000 pixels on one side. The product description couldn't include personal information or my shop policies. My online shop for my own website needed a policy page. The products I sold needed to be on the homepage and the layout had to be consistent in its presentation. When I say it was a six month process, I mean it took Amazon six months to approve my application in 2011. In 2014 Amazon removed the restrictions and guidelines. An influx of sellers arrived. I was also confronted locally with a lot of people jumping into the resell business. It didn't matter that I was passionate about kicks, or that

I made my own shoes and ran a website, any person locally who had the money was buying shoes from the same brick and mortar retailers. This influx of new buyers in Memphis meant that a reseller had to have serious connections to get what was readily available. Where in the 2000s I could walk into the stores and grab anything sitting on the shelves, by 2014 everyone was trying to get paid. I chose not to pay managers and employees to get inventory for me. In 2014 I was nailed in two ways, locally and with Amazon's loosening of restrictions.

My fifth year on Amazon was 2015. I was able to adjust to the new reality that everyone was a reseller by completely abandoning my routine of visiting retail shops in Memphis. I expanded my store reach to locations in Mississippi. That's an entirely different story, but what's important is that my sales increased on Amazon although Amazon had also during the previous year begin to enforce brand registries. I became more of a wholesaler than a reseller in 2015 and 2016. In 2015 my Amazon revenue was: **$317,994.11**; a slight increase from 2014, but still nowhere near my first three years. All of the work I did in Mississippi was disrupted by Nike's Consumer Direct Offense. The small accounts I was working with were basically pushed out of business. A small three store chain lost their Nike account because they hadn't redesigned their stores. There was more to it, but this was the reason given. A seven store chain dropped to 5 stores. This chain had redesigned their stores, but never could make the money they invested on the redesign. Nike had increased the number of shoes they were making and the urban accounts that relied on Jordan Brand had so much inventory that they couldn't sell it all. What was a bigger issue is that the chain had to increase the amount of non-Retro models and the amount of apparel to get the shoes that sold better. The seven store chain, like I said, became a five store chain and eventually sold outright to another company. From 2014 to 2015 I had been able to survive because I had access as the online shop for the two Mississippi based small chains. I had to find a different source of inventory heading into 2016.

My sixth year on Amazon was 2016: **$258,552.72**.

By 2017 I was out of business. My sneaker resale had collapsed under the weight of bad decisions and the shift in sneaker e-commerce. I will get into the Amazon policies that really contributed to the collapse of my business in the next paragraph. When you take into consideration that In 2016 StockX and GOAT launched and Amazon had almost every major brand in its registry, the digital shift was starting and I knew it, but I kept pushing as if Amazon would cure my problems.

In 2017 I took what little money I had and I tried StockX. In 2015 however, I saw the writing on the wall and shifted my entire business plan. I knew Amazon was killing me, but I pushed forward trying to scrape by. I had left the Memphis market for two years. During that time there were more resellers than ever. Getting sneakers was more difficult of course, but it was one moment on Amazon that completely killed my business. I couldn't prevent the collapse on the financial side.

In 2015 I wholesaled over 400,000 dollars in shoes. That wasn't by choice. I was forced by Amazon to sell shoes that I could have made three times the amount of money selling the sneakers myself. How did Amazon force me to wholesale? I have to explain this in its own section, but here is a bit of information that should scare you if you're an Amazon Seller Central Marketplace store, at the end of 2016 Amazon was doing work on the back end of Seller Central. I had worked out a relationship with a local store to place the inventory on my shop. This was perfect because I didn't have any inventory and I still had just enough money to buy shoes. All I had to do was visit the store when something sold. It took a considerable amount of time to put the products up on my Amazon shop. I woke up one morning in November just before Black Friday, the busiest time of year for sellers and my entire inventory had been switched to inactive.

Now, don't think I discovered this right away. Inside of the Amazon dashboard the products still showed as listed. Amazon had implemented a rule for all marketplace stores that they had to offer Free Shipping in a different way in the settings. I thought I had my settings correct, but after a week I didn't have any sales. Entering into December of 2016 I kept looking at my online shop and adjusting prices. As I adjust prices some sales flowed in, but it was still slow. There is a link in the dashboard to compare your prices to other stores. I clicked the link and realized my products weren't showing up. I wrote Amazon Help and started a case. They eventually got back to me and explained that everything should have been working fine. In the meantime I discovered that I had to recreate all of my listings. Over 500 shoe listings had to be created again. By the time I finished I had basically missed the shopping season.

In 2015 December I made $41,948.33

In 2016 December I made $34,117.31

To make matters worse after I had recreated my entire store, Amazon reset information in the system and my entire store was 'erased'. It wasn't that my Amazon dashboard disappeared, Amazon had made every listing inactive and simply adding the product didn't fix the issue. Every listing had to be recreated. In January of 2017 I realized what I always understood and I left Amazon.

Amazon was my pimp and the flaws beat me to death; I just didn't see it happening. Actually I did see it happening, but like Out-Kast said, "A junkie is a junkie, 365," and I was a fiend. I was a junkie going back for more although I knew what I was doing to my business. Here is why.

Chapter 12

Learning the Hard Way

It seems that I'm placing all of my problems at the feet of Amazon. The reality is my naiveté in small business was part of it. I didn't have any mentors in business. From the moment I made my first shoe with Sho-Shot in 2006 and then when I created my next shoe company in ARCH in 2009, I had never taken a business class. When I grossed my first million on Amazon, I was learning on the fly. I had trusted my own research in operating an Amazon shop. I had read books about becoming a millionaire and how you could build a great business on Amazon. All of those books were wrong. The way you build a business is via owning your platform. As I said earlier though, some businesses can utilize Amazon effectively, but this is why I wouldn't recommend it.

Amazon only pays out every 14 days, a bi-monthly payment which has a wire transfer processing time of 3 days. This one thing is huge. During my time on Amazon I had access to entire store inventories. I set myself up as a liquidator for small accounts. As the smaller accounts began to disappear I tapped into business relationships with small chains. This allowed me access to storerooms and I used my Amazon store as the online store for a small chain. It was perfect. Everything I made was pure profit. I didn't have to buy product outright since I was granted a store discount instead of a paycheck by the chain.

As the inventory sold I packed and shipped through Amazon. This was great as long as I kept 10-20,000 in my business account. The problem was a problem most would enjoy; on Amazon I could sell 10-20,000 dollars in one week. The problem was I didn't have an endless supply of money. Every week I would have to place my store on vacation because I would run out of money. Is this clear? I would sell so much in the first week that I wouldn't have money left for the second week between the payouts from Amazon.

Here is the first reason Amazon is a trap for small businesses: Growth happens quickly and if you don't have the cash to continue purchasing inventory your business can collapse. How? While Seller Central/Amazon Marketplace pays every two weeks, any other platform a seller sells through the money arrives immediately. eBay transfers the payment to your PayPal account. Kixify uses PayPal. Your own website you are paid immediately. StockX uses PayPal or your bank account and they have an option named "Early Payouts" where the moment you drop your sneakers off with UPS they begin the payout transaction and your money is in your account by the end of the day. Square pays out at the end of each day. I'm sure the picture is a bit clearer, but if it isn't let me explain.

Amazon's payout happens every 17 days. This means that if you are like me and you have about 20,000 on hand at all times you can go through that in 4 days. With a profit margin of about 20% that's 4000.00 dollars that you will be paid in 17 days. If you had your money immediately you would make $8,000 dollars every 8 days, $12,000 every 12 days... you get the picture. Selling on Amazon stifles your growth and turns a 40,000 dollar month into an 8% a month profit margin. I'm sure you're asking, "Why is the profit margin so low?" If you are only being paid every 17 days, that's the obvious issue, but the truth is I was a reseller. I was buying the product from an account selling to me at slightly above wholesale. This means my margins were already gone. Kixify charges 8% fees. eBay is 12.75% fees including PayPal. StockX at the highest seller level is 11% fees. Amazon rings up at your *monthly service charge* for Seller Central plus 15%. This meant my profit margin was basically gone before I even started. When I first entered Amazon the marketplace was a lot less crowded and the margins were better. There was also less competition locally. I had been reselling shoes since 2004 part time at flea markets and on eBay and I basically had the run of the city as far as buying. By 2012 people were watching me and talking and I was teaching other people. When those people undercut my action, my margins decreased. The more people that were involved, the margins were lower. Amazon was always a problem that progressively became worse.

In 2014 an influx of eBay sellers migrated to Amazon. My margins decreased. What's worse is that Amazon allowed counterfeit sellers to pop up and with the brand registry allowing brands more control, it was a perfect storm and as I said at the beginning of this book Nike's Consumer Direct Offense was set in motion in 2014 in a much bigger way. Remember when I asked the question, "What if Nike's CDO was intentional disruption?" Nike unleashed a flood of product into the market. What happens when there is too much of a product?

Thermal Map Foamposites and Silver Camo Foamposites

I'm mentioning these Nike Foamposite products because they signaled the beginning of the end for the resale of the Nike Foamposite and it was also the time where small accounts could finally get the Nike Foamposite which was traditionally a sneaker designated for House of Hoops or top tiered accounts for Nike. The Thermal Map and Silver Camo Foamposites ended up being some of the worst shoes ever created by Nike. A lot of people within sneaker culture even gave the Thermal Map Foamposites the nickname 'herpes' foams because of the red blotch designs on the shoes. For me it was worse because I was doing well enough on Amazon, or so I thought, that I gave a store owner cash for over 200 pair. The owner sold every pair to me at 175 a pair. The retail price for those Foamposites was 230 and 250. I thought this would be a bonus for my shop. It wasn't. For the first time since the Foamposite had come back, the shoes tanked. No one wanted the shoes. I was out of my liquid cash on hand and the shoes didn't sell for a year and when they finally were gone the average price for every pair sold was right at 180 with Amazon taking 15%.

2014 was the year that everything for Nike began to change. Nike had begun to discuss removing Futures as evidence of growth. The removal of Futures finally did occur in 2016. When Nike finally created their brand registry on Amazon in 2017 I understood the seriousness of this move and the direct to consumer strategy better than anyone. The brand registry in conjunction with Nike's CDO was a direct influence on the ability of third party marketplaces to be born. I had been caught, not in the wake, but in the undertow. I was spinning out of control towards the propellers at the back of a Nike aircraft carrier.

Chapter 13

How Amazon Opened the Door for 3rd Party

I can't stress how important it is to understand how Amazon was the first and last straw that broke my back. In order to explain how a site like StockX or GOAT has become so successful I have to really establish the inherent issues that exist for sellers on Amazon. There are problems with all third party platforms, but my most recent experience lies with Amazon Seller Central. Amazon added so many sellers in 2014 that it was harder to earn the "Buy Box". Amazon also forced all sellers to adhere to their return policies. Originally my store had its own return policies. I kept my returns to 7 days and "no returns" on exclusive, limited product. When Amazon forced all stores to function *"like"* Amazon around 2014-2015 my return rates rose from 10% to 30%. 30%!!!! When you take into consideration that to compete on Amazon you had to offer Free Shipping to win the "Buy Box"[37], the 15% fees, the 17 day payout of your own money, the moment I signed up for Amazon, I was dead. I just didn't know it.

This is a side note: To add insult to injury Amazon later partnered with a business named Payability. Payablity used a merchant code to access your Amazon Marketplace account. The company scrapes your account information and they can pay your money from Amazon daily, for a fee. Amazon is almost a trillion dollar company and they are the only third party platform that doesn't pay you the money you've made daily. They then have the audacity to partner with a business that charges you to access your money faster! I had to write this because the sheer absurdity of the business arrangement should be gold for third party platforms looking to court sellers away from the biggest e-commerce platform in the world. As a matter of

[37] The Buy Box is the small box where the price shows up on Amazon. The store that wins the Buy Box usually has the lowest price and free shipping. In 2011 the algorithm used to include the stores feedback, but that changed around 2014.

fact that is the crack in the armor where businesses can attack Amazon.

Back to my explanation of Amazon issues:

The returns on Amazon were terrible. Many shoes would come back damaged and very often returns were a case of buyer's remorse. In resale many of the big profit shoes you sell are limited release models. The problem with those models as 2016 rolled around, they were harder to come by and with new marketplaces popping up the shoes were no longer holding their value. A shoe you could sell on Day 1 at $300.00, in a week instead of the shoe increasing in price, it would adjust to the new market at $200.00 If you paid $160.00 plus tax for that shoe, after 15% and free shipping you would take a loss or you would have to hold the shoe for months which is still a loss, after a customer returned the shoe. On Amazon, the shoes could be returned for up to 30 days. They would arrive back worn and you would have a challenge on your hands that you would lose and Amazon would refund the money. Amazon always sides with the buyer.

An additional problem is that Amazon has a higher rate of chargebacks[38] and fraud claims because of the sheer volume of people using the platform. I once had a buyer purchase six pairs of Air Jordan 4 Retro Cavs at resell prices. The buyer probably thought they could flip them and make a profit. When it didn't happen the buyer filed a chargeback claim. Amazon took the price per pair and pulled it from my funds that were to be transferred. That was around 250 a pair. Remember I was only transferring out around 4000 dollars in profit. They kept 1200 in the 'air' for over a month. That was a case I "won" but the customer was still able to return 4 pair. The shoes had lost their resale value completely. At the time it didn't bother me, but as I look back on this moment and the numerous occasions I had claims and chargebacks, it's a wonder how I made it six years.

This is overwhelming isn't it? Remember I started this with a discussion on how I would have to shut down my store because I would run out of money? Now factor in the returns and you have a smaller profit margin. I wholesaled almost half a million dollars in

[38] On Amazon a customer will often pay for an item and after the product arrives they will file a chargeback claiming that they didn't order the product. The problem is they would also state that they never received the product. Amazon immediately takes these funds and places them on hold. Amazon almost always gives the buyer the funds and the seller typically takes a loss.

sneakers because every week I ran out of money and by the time I got the money instead of a $4,000.00 dollar profit, it was about $3,000.00. That's $3,000 a month on sales of $40,000 a month. That's a 7.5% profit because Amazon only paid out every 17 days… once a month. Just in case you were wondering why I wholesaled over 400,000 dollars in sneakers, remember I was functioning as the online store for a small chain. These were shoes that I could have sold if I could pay for the shoes immediately. Unfortunately the small chain was having so many issues meeting payroll that my work as the online shop and wholesale outlet was often required to meet payroll. The CEO of the chain wouldn't allow me to continue to sell on Amazon and build a "tab". He wanted the cash in hand. I was taking entire shipments of shoes and sending them to sellers in other states. This was a direct reflection of the issues many smaller chains and retailers have who are not addressing their digital strategies.

My goal in writing this section is to explain how the digital shift in retail sales is the single most important factor in continued growth for all segments of retail.

People tout Amazon as the path to financial freedom, and I'm saying it's a slow road to death, what can be done at retail and online to offset a reliance on Amazon or any third party platform? Honestly, there isn't much because when you're small the amount of work needed to direct traffic to your site is extensive and very hard to accomplish as a one to two person team, but it can be done. Sneaker retailers aren't small. They are multimillion dollar businesses who don't have the time or just don't care about looking at the variety of situations I'm presenting in this book.

In 2015 when I saw everything crumbling, I began building my own platform via content. The plan has been about slow growth, but that's how it works with a 1-2 person team building two websites. Since 2015 the website traffic growth on AHN has been over 6000%. Both websites are earning revenue and garnering considerable traffic. Why is this important?

Retailers are in a position where they are battling for eyes against social media feeds, they are battling against brands that see direct to consumer as a growth area, and retail is fighting against an agile, cash cow in Amazon. The sooner retailers and small business people recognize that their digital platform is critical in continuing growth, the more likely it becomes that they don't go bankrupt like I did.

Chapter 14

Nike Owns Sneaker Traffic

The Nike Consumer Direct Offense creates a double edged sword for wholesale accounts. Nike dominates retail. Without Nike a retail store has to be really unique in their presentation to drive foot traffic, most stores are not unique. I saw firsthand how not having a Nike account hurts a store with Memphis' only Sheikh sneaker store. Sheikh did not have a Nike account in their Memphis location. The store also suffered from the most uninspired floor plan in the mall. There wasn't any originality or anything interesting. Without Nike there wasn't any reason for people to visit and check out the small selection of footwear Sheikh did carry. It wasn't that Sheikh failed because they didn't carry Nike, they failed because they didn't sell what they had very well. The store was wack, but if I'm being honest it didn't look that much different from every other store in the mall. The location was smaller and had less apparel, but the only difference in Sheikh and the other 5 sneaker stores in the mall was Nike.

Most stores have a problem with merchandising. If you've been inside of one store, you've been inside of all stores. The same repetitious store layout does not inspire interaction. The employees are not paid very well either. *Low pay, long hours* is the motto at sneaker retail and this creates a rotating door of employees who don't even know the product. This lack of knowledge of what is being carried contributes to poor sell through. Brand stores are better suited to sell their products.

Since Nike knows its value the brand continuously pushes out footwear and apparel to feed its machine. 30,000 shoes a day are shipped out of Nike's supply centers. Wholesale accounts are packed to the brim because new releases arrive every week. Many of the shoes sit and accounts that can return to vendor do so and take on new inventory. Stores that choose not to *return to vendor*, discount their shoes.

When Nike loads an account down and takes inventory back on an RTV, this is not a loss for Nike. Those shoes end up in one of Nike's many doors, factory stores or clearance stores. The clearance store becomes a distribution center for resale; creating online competition for Nike's wholesale accounts. Retailers have resorted to heavy discount tactics to sell product. Those discounts at stores supply a *secondary* supply chain for resale. The problem is since Nike implemented their CDO they are opening more stores than their wholesale accounts; this means Nike is *competing* with their wholesale accounts.

I discussed this earlier, but I'm emphasizing why resale exists. I don't want to simplify the issue into a problem and solution based on *company website traffic*, but a problem requires analysis and AHN (ARCH x Housakicks Network) intentionally set out in 2018 to understand how resale can exist when retail websites with the same sneakers being resold on third party have the products readily available.

Initially Tayib and I chalked up resale to *conscious consumers* vs *unconscious consumers*. The conscious consumer is an active comparison shopper. They spend time researching a product before buying. The unconscious consumer tends to have a sense of urgency. This consumer will search online and instead of taking the time to visit the brand or the store website they click on the search links on Google and Bing, they read and then make a decision to purchase. When an unconscious consumer searches for products what do they discover? That consumer discovers sneaker sites like Solecollector, Nice Kicks, Kicks on Fire, Hypebeast and other sneaker culture websites. On a small scale they discover my site ARCH because I've created over 400 videos in the last year for as many sneakers that I could. Those videos rank high on Google Search which has led to traffic to the site. When I say that retailers are leaving money on the table, this is not speculation.

The store on Housakicks.com works as a drop ship site. All of the products listed on the site are purchased from online sneaker shops and brick and mortar locations and shipped directly to the consumer. Very often Tayib never touches the product. He sells the product through his site or through eBay at a markup. This is not unique to Housakicks. There isn't any reason Tayib's dropship method should work on his site, or on eBay. His resale strategy (which will later be classified as the variable because he used more than one location to resale shoes) should not be capable if retailers were actually working just as hard as sneaker culture websites to generate traffic.

Think about it, why would retail leave revenue on the table when people are out there looking for the product?

From 2015 to 2018 the AHN sites went from zero online orders to producing orders via the sites. The AHN sites don't garner any traffic in comparison to larger websites. Hypebeast with their e-commerce, HBX, averages 14 Million visits a month but combined AHN's website numbers rival small brick and mortar sneaker stores. Because we write on a daily basis we are able to earn money via our sites. Foot Locker, Finish Line, Hibbett Sports, DTLR already have search because they have the products, imagine if they coupled that with content.

My resale strategy took place on one platform. (It will be listed as the control in the resale experiment.) ARCH has been working through StockX and compiling information. Housakicks has been utilizing the drop ship method. This comparison and contrast experiment is the first of its kind. The sales have helped to inform this book, but once again, how does this help small retail or anyone reading?

Online consumers are not looking at retailers who own accounts with Nike as the first place to visit for kicks. Why are consumers going to eBay, Amazon, StockX, Kixify, HBX and GOAT on a large scale and visiting sites like AHN on a small scale instead of visiting KicksUSA, Jimmy Jazz, City Gear, DTLR, and Shoe Palace which are account holders with brands?

It is becoming increasingly difficult in the sneaker industry to take traffic away from Nike. With the capital flowing into digital third party marketplaces via investment those platforms are utilizing Google Ads and Facebook Ads to drive traffic. There is a war for keywords and small retailers are losing.

At the same time that third party/pureplay sites are battling for consumers via ad spend, Nike has taken the backdoor to cut into the traffic being generated by online websites. As a part of Nike's CDO efforts the brand has launched *SNKRS, Nike News and air.jordan.com.* These subsites of Nike are functioning in the same manner as the sneaker blogs that dominate search for sneakers. What does this mean for the retailers that carry the brand?

Nike has shifted gears from an advertising company that makes sneakers, to a media company that makes sneakers. In changing their strategy the company has their eyes set more on fighting Complex than on adidas. What does this mean? Complex has the potential to be a disruptive force in footwear and apparel if it decides to do so. Nike realizes this and they are responding accordingly by launching their own news platforms. Interestingly enough adidas has followed suit and Under Armour has followed this pattern. The only companies failing to grasp the importance of building content and news sites to increase interaction with their consumer base are retail outlets. Foot Locker once used *Foot Locker Unlocked*, but that site has been dormant for three years. Nike increased their output over the last three years via various media platforms, Foot Locker decreased output, but Nike and Foot Locker have a symbiotic relationship so Foot Locker can kind of get away with the lack of content being produced. The rest of the industry does not have that relationship with Nike.

Don't get me wrong a blog isn't going to fix retail or a brand. It's a component in a marketing strategy; when utilized correctly it's the solder that connects the wires to the motherboard. Businesses have to invest in every aspect of the operation, but what happens if the smallest thing in a circuit turns into a cold joint or a broken solder point? It can't be seen and a tech spends an inordinate amount of time replacing the processor and trying to track down the problem. The tech might even replace the entire motherboard which will solve the issue, but at a much greater expense than making sure the small solder joint was bright and shiny.

Does a bright and shiny content management system matter? Yes.

Chapter 15

Rewriting Business: Social Media vs Search

I began building the ARCH x Housakicks Network because I followed my own advice in understanding the power of content in driving traffic to websites. I had written a book in 2015 titled *The 30 Day Project: How Daily Dedication Can Lead to Something Amazing*. The book was based on my goal to write short posts on business for 30 days straight. Those 30 posts became the foundation for the new business plan for ARCH and the backbone of the book. I knew that I had made mistakes in creating my business and I had so much in my head that the only way to get everything out was to spend an hour everyday writing about all of the errors I made. The biggest mistake was my overreliance on third party and my failure to invest in my own website.

My Amazon Marketplace store created a false sense of security. I thought I was making so much money that I didn't see the point of spending time developing my website. I wasted a ton of energy and money in trying to build up my social media following. I paid for Facebook Ads and reached over a 1000 followers on the platform and as soon as I stopped paying for the ads, the interaction and *likes* fell through the floor. I was writing on my site about what I was doing to sell my ARCH running shoes, but I didn't even list the products I was selling on Amazon *for sale* on my website. Here is something truly absurd. I knew that building my site was smart. I had written another book on the importance of building a site to launch a business. Although my income was dropping on Amazon, I was making six figures still. I thought I was doing so well that instead of actually creating my own e-commerce shop, I built my e-commerce shop into an affiliate site[39]. I think I need a new paragraph to show how *intelligently stupid* I was.

I was writing on my website about my shoe company ARCH and how I created my brand. I set up my online shop, but instead of listing the products I sold on Amazon, I created the product page on the ARCH site and I placed an affiliate link to the products I was selling on Amazon. I hope that's clear. I was *stupid smart.* I thought this was genius. Since I was winning the Buy Box on Amazon I would get a 4-6% commission on items that I was selling on Amazon. I was earning an extra 100 dollars a month on sales through my site from affiliate links. Why is this stupid?

If people were visiting my site and clicking through, they were *discovering the products* on my site. If I simply listed the same inventory on my site who knows how many visitors I could have converted into buyers. You know what my fees would have been? 2.75% PayPal fees and free shipping would have been my only cost. Instead I ran my own site as an affiliate site to my Amazon store because I thought

[39] Affiliate programs allow the owner of a website to share products via e-mail, or hyperlinks from a site like Amazon. When the link is clicked and an item is purchased the person who shared the link earns a percentage of the sales total.

I was tricking the system. The reality was I was losing an opportunity to capture e-mail sign ups and customer information that I could use to inform my customers of new inventory. I gave all of my power to Amazon although I knew how to build engagement on my site.

I knew that the best way to generate enough consistent traffic and visitors to the site was to create daily content. I was writing on my site about starting a footwear brand. At the same time I was creating a database of sneakers with affiliate links. Those sneakers were being indexed and were searchable via Google and Bing. That was the reason I was earning affiliate revenue. People were finding the sneaker listings.

The most important information I can write is *website traffic is dominated by search*. Many retail companies and brands are spending considerable money on social media. The social sites have begun to monetize by creating retail options within their platforms. An Instagram marketplace or Facebook marketplace introduces the same issues for brands and retailers that I experienced on Amazon. As social sites incorporate "stores" on their platforms the seller in all likelihood won't capture the information, the social platform will. There will be fees associated with the social media marketplaces. Those fees along with fluctuating ad purchase prices on social media create a separate issue; an issue I encountered on Amazon.

When Amazon began adding more sellers, product discovery was made more difficult. I began using Amazon Ads to funnel traffic to my Amazon store. This worked wonders for my small brand as I actually sold out of my ARCH running shoes in this way. The problem was my own brand had razor thin margins. The cost to acquire customers fluctuated from 2-4 dollars with Amazon Ads. Once again I thought this was okay, but it wasn't. As small businesses begin building social sites, even if those social sites create online shops, the fees incurred and the fact that as algorithms change for discovery on social media more ads will be needed to increase engagement. Social is valuable, but a business will still have to convert their social followers to buyers at some point.

How does this information on redeveloping my business plan fit the book? I'm trying to explain the importance of building a CMS based website for brands, retail and small business. Right now marketing is *social media and influencers*.

As brands and retailers spend money on influencers and social media ads, the results are qualitative and measuring the value of an influencer is often not very straightforward. There are reports on the effectiveness of ad spend with social media platforms like Facebook.

In 2018 adidas suspended all ads running on Facebook. I wrote a post on the matter[40]:

> It would seem that a 20 Billion dollar a year company like adidas wouldn't have any trouble connecting to its primary fan. The reality is that every brand, big or small, is faced with the growing popularity of social media and how it occupies the mind and time of every person with a phone. Every brand has to figure out how to get people to see what they are creating. Then they have to figure out how to convert a browser into a buyer.

[40] https://arch-usa.com/adidas-paused-its-facebook-ads-via-digiday-marketing/

What's interesting however is that when you take a moment to research how people get to purchasing channels (Locations where you buy stuff) the numbers are fairly consistent across the board for engagement from social:

Brand website traffic: Search vs Social (search is traffic that arrives via Google, Bing or search engines, social is traffic that arrives via social media sites like Facebook or Instagram).

Nike.com traffic – Search vs Social: 45.35% vs 7.4%

adidas.com traffic – Search vs Social: 47.29% vs 6.9%

Under Armour traffic – Search vs Social: 40.39% vs 3.39%

Now within these numbers there is a deeper analysis available in regard to paid vs organic search and the same within social.

We are at a time where brands are failing to understand "branding" in the new arena. Simply making people aware of you no longer carries the brand to the consumer. Slapping content all over the place does very little long term as trends are likes waves in the ocean, they rise, fall, and riptides come out of nowhere to change everything in an instant. In other words, social media strategies should begin to be placed into a category of temporary promotional solutions. If social is the strategy, it will take constant investment and content creation because you lose the long term strategy aligned with the traffic source that is the best for every brand, search.

If you have a campaign that requires a lot of people to know about it immediately, then use social. If your goal is to build an audience via a consistent and long term strategy it's going to take a lot more than a Facebook ad. There is considerable evidence of how deep the drop off is once a Facebook ad ends. The drop

> off is the distance from a cliff to the valley floor and it is Grand Canyon status. adidas was right to pause their campaigns as my research shows that their traffic as it relates to social is better generated through Twitter and Reddit.

The reason I used a long form quote above is to establish that even a brand as big as adidas finds it difficult to navigate the new digital marketing landscape. Nike, unlike adidas, can get away with experimentation in marketing via social media; but as social platforms begin establishing ecommerce shops, utilizing social media marketplaces will carry the same risks that social media *ads* carry.

It is in the benefit of the social media platform to force *marketplaces* to utilize ads to promote their stores. Facebook Ads and Instagram Ads are required to reach customers on social when originally a retailer or brand could simply post on their social media pages to engage with their followers. While brands have the ability to create Instagram Marketplaces, as Nike has done in the UK, the fees incurred by retailers who decide to use social marketplaces in the future will not be sustainable.

Retailers in the long term have to do what Nike has done in creating CMS sites. Retailers have to literally reverse engineer a site like StockX. StockX was born as a website which analyzed sales data on eBay to find the shoes reselling at the highest price. The site, named Campless, provided a stock market styled database and it garnered considerable traffic. Campless then utilized the traffic on their site to put together an investible platform where they could translate the visitors to the site into sellers. As I have mentioned throughout this book StockX now ranks higher for online traffic than almost every brick and mortar sneaker retailer. Sneaker chains need to follow Nike, StockX, GOAT, Stadium Goods, and boutique shops like BAIT and KITH in becoming more than just static, product based sites. Retailers need to create media companies dedicated to driving traffic to their e-commerce platforms. Why should both small and big businesses do this? Social media and influencers are short term solutions to website traffic. As I listed in the long quote above most traffic derives from *Direct visits and Search*.

Direct traffic consists of visitors who have a site bookmarked or who type the name of the site into the URL to visit.

Search traffic consists of customers who utilize a search engine to find information on products.

It would seem that spending time on long form content via websites is counter to all of the work in social media a company like Nike has been doing. The interesting thing is that Nike has discovered what I discovered in 2015 when I changed my business plan. Content is king and queen; the introduction of new tech and products provides information for a machine constantly looking for the next new thing.

Chapter 16

The Transition

When I was selling on Amazon I directed traffic away from my own site to my Amazon marketplace store. I wasn't consistent in updating the site. My website was home to articles about ARCH and how I launched the company. I had an online store but all of my products linked to my Amazon store via Amazon Associates, an affiliate program that gave me a return on *clicks through*. Like I said, I thought it was genius. I would get 4-6% back on products that I was selling on my shop. Amazon was taking 15%. Amazon did not allow me to write to my customer and I had no customer database. I did not own the information of people I sold to, Amazon did. My website was effective, but ineffective. In 2015 I began writing about utilizing Facebook Ads and I began analyzing the sneaker market in detail on ARCH. My site grew from 300 visits per month in 2015 to 3000 visits per month in 2016. I sat down and wrote a business plan and redesigned my partner's website Housakicks.com to form a network. My goal was to mimic *Complex* and create a series of sneaker sites that would provide more in-depth coverage of the sneaker industry. Housakicks.com was struggling. Tayib at the time was paying a developer to run his site, but he wasn't getting the results he wanted.

When he reached out to me in 2015 he wanted to pay me to run his site. I wanted to start building a network. The timing was perfect and instead of charging him to redesign and develop his site, I told him I would teach him to run the site himself and at the same time we could work together to create a sneaker network that wrote deeper discussions on the sneaker industry. Tayib had been in resale for years and we had common ground. In the redesign I made Housakicks the "sneakerhead" site. ARCH became the business site for the sneaker industry. Combined in 2018, ARCH and Housakicks hit a combined 150,000 page views per month which has enabled the network (Housakicks) to begin selling shoes via the websites. Housakicks earns considerable affiliate revenue and ad revenue. Later in this book I will discuss the yearlong experiment on third party resale performed by Tayib and I. Housakicks has begun selling footwear consistently on the site.

In 2016 and 2017 ARCH sold kicks on a small scale, but I intentionally disrupted my growth by completely erasing my site and recreating the site. I had to do this because of my time on Amazon. When Amazon required me to make the store the homepage of my site, I shifted my blog for the site to a subsite. In order to grow AHN I needed to make the content the primary site. The result of our work on AHN has been eye-opening and as many resellers have fallen to all of the shifts in sneaker retail, Tayib and I realized how important it was for us to change gears and focus on the sites.

How does this help small retailers and you who are reading?

As sellers are moving back and forth on a variety of resale platforms, customers are overlooking the websites where most *resellers* are buying their products. That sentence might be a bit confusing. When Tayib, who lives in Maryland, and I, living in Memphis, buy footwear that we are selling through our websites or on third party platforms, we visit store locations in our area. The entire business strategy for resellers, all resellers except those with considerable discounts via Nike or Foot Locker, is to scour stores for the best deals. Stores are operating on the premise of "sales drive foot traffic" when resellers are operating on the premise of "people online want these shoes". After a year of keeping track of how much could be grossed on third party using two strategies, the reseller is correct; which means retail outlets and brands are leaving money on the table in order to liquidate older inventory.

Chapter 17

Can Content Counter CDO?

ARCH is a not a very big website, but it holds the key to the digital strategy for small retail, and for all of retail. In countering the direct to consumer approach by brands and the encroachment by third party marketplaces, businesses have to invest in merchandising and in-store experiences at physical locations. Online businesses need to build long-term solutions that will sustain the website longer than a company can run an ad.

One of the biggest issues brick and mortar sneaker stores have is that their websites are static. There really is not a reason for people to visit retail sites daily because the updates on the sites are primarily product updates and if I'm honest, the websites in many cases are terrible. The search is flawed and the ease of finding what is desired is non-existent. In tech terms the User Interface of most retail chain sneaker websites are poor.

I had a visitor to ARCH leave a comment, "… I recently tried to buy a new pair of Under Armor Curry 6 shoes online from Foot Locker as it appears Under Armor does not sell through Amazon. It proved impossible due to Foot Locker's poor online shopping experience. I chose instead to buy an alternative product through Amazon. No problems."[41]

When compared to third party sites like StockX or Kixify the difference really becomes noticeable. When a new shoe is released for traditional websites, traffic should increase. The company will typically have a splash graphic on the home page of the site directing a visitor to the latest release. Traffic for traditional retail e-commerce does not have a problem on a release day. That is not where the problems lie. When there isn't a new shoe being released is where traditional retail experiences problems with driving customer en-

---

[41] https://arch-usa.com/2-reasons-nike-selling-amazon-will-disrupt-foot-locker-finish-line-retail-outlets/#comment-4308146347

gagement and visits. If the latest 'hyped' product isn't being dropped retail websites won't typically garner any traffic unless the company is running Google Ads. A customer has to be actively looking to make a purchase to visit a traditional retail site.

On third party platforms and independent boutiques like KITH a customer will drop in on the blog because KITH might be posting pics of a recent photo shoot or dropping creative pictures of upcoming releases. A third party site like the Kixify online shop gets daily traffic because the primary website *Kicks on Fire* posts between 1-5 new articles daily. In those articles there are links to the online shop where the product can be purchased. *Kicks on Fire* gets 2.4 million visits per month; and Kixify, the online shop for the site, gets another 826,000 visits per month. I have never seen an ad for *Kicks on Fire or Kixify*. Traditional retail relies solely on release day for traffic, but the new release or upcoming sneaker release conversation is dominated by sneaker lifestyle sites. Most people reading Complex or Hypebeast are not the people that traditional retail websites are targeting, but the domination of search by sneaker culture and their online shops shouldn't be influential when a person sits down to look for a pair of shoes online. Unfortunately the sneaker culture and lifestyle websites do dominate search and this has contributed to the rise of third party e-commerce sites. It's a natural progression especially with the amount of money flowing from venture capitalists and investment firms.

When you contrast e-commerce sites of smaller boutiques like KITH, Bait and Bodega, the difference in quality and content is night and day. Boutiques are continuously updating customers via their website content management systems on old and new footwear releasing, music, art, fashion, food and anything that is remotely associated with the lifestyle around kicks. Smaller boutiques are not the only companies taking advantage of creating content for their sites. As mentioned earlier, Nike in the last year has introduced as a part of their CDO push CMS sites that look and function like blogs for the brand.

Nike and independent boutiques are implementing long form content into their marketing strategies. It's obvious that Nike is benefitting from this. Are the indie stores benefitting? The pureplay Kicks

On Fire/Kixify combination is evidence of the tactic working. In 2017 the owner of the site, Furqan Khan, landed on the Forbes *30 under 30* list[42].

Kicks On Fire is a gateway to the e-commerce platform Kixify which was designed for third party sellers. Comparing that site to traditional brick and mortar is problematic. Kixify isn't a physical store, but it could be. What isn't problematic is how smaller independent sneaker stores are doing with online traffic?

Kith is a small chain with three stores. Their website traffic is 1.86 Million a month.

Bodega is a boutique with one store. Their website traffic is 613,000 a month.

Bait is a chain with seven stores. Their website traffic is 403,000 a month.

In a previous chapter I listed monthly traffic for a number of sites. Look at the website traffic for City Gear, DTLR and Villa on

[42] https://www.kicksonfire.com/kixify-founder-forbes-30-under-30/

page 37, chains with considerably more locations, and smaller boutiques are garnering more website traffic for one reason, consistent content updates.

A quick analysis of Jimmy Jazz shows that they already have a considerable amount of website traffic. I chose Jimmy Jazz because this company, of all of the 'urban' accounts for Nike has adjusted their in store layout and they've also invested into their online layout. At 44.3% Direct traffic, 31.79% Search and 12.39% Social, it would appear that Jimmy Jazz is doing everything needed to grow their e-commerce. However, a closer inspection shows that although the chain is doing considerable work, there are opportunities for adjustments to be made. Direct traffic could be higher, but search is where the real work could take place. At this point, JimmyJazz.com is currently at 82% Organic and 18% Paid for search. Jimmy Jazz is battling for keywords within Google AdWords. Finish Line, Foot Locker, Nike, adidas, and StockX, are all battling for keywords which drives up the purchase price of ads.

Continuing to look at Jimmy Jazz, a quick estimate is that 360,000 visits to JimmyJazz.com are paid visits arriving from ads. "The average conversion rate in Google Ads on mobile across all industries is 3.48% on the search network and 0.72% on the display network." This quote is for Search and display[43] ads in the Google Network.

In all categories for ads, retail has a 3.11% conversion. It appears that Jimmy Jazz is using Conversant Media. Without any working knowledge of how Conversant is guiding traffic to the site, I cannot put a price on how much the advertising budget is for the company. I do know that at 3.11% conversion on an estimated 360,000 visits equates to 11,196 visits monthly from customers who may or may not purchase an item from the site. These numbers are primarily for the sake of discussion as I have no real measurement of what is occurring with Jimmy Jazz. These statistics derive from research done using Similarweb. It could be that the company has an effective strategy and does not need to adjust any part of the digital platform; which would render this section moot.

---

[43] https://www.smartinsights.com/paid-search-marketing-ppc/paid-search-display-network/google-adwords-conversion-rate-averages-by-industry-infographic/

However, as I stated earlier in this paper, all retailers have a unique opportunity to be at the forefront of content creation which will have to become a part of every business strategy, not just retail, every business.

Chapter 18

The Digital Shift & the Cash Customer

Social media is currently the *perceived* best option for engaging the consumer. Influencers on social media channels are now garnering deals to namedrop and talk about brands and stores. The problem with the reliance on influencers and the reliance on social media is the amount of content required to control the conversation with any consistency is a quantitative and qualitative nightmare. Measuring traffic from Instagram, Facebook or Twitter can be done, but the measurement means very little as social media posts provide momentary gains. Instagram may be working on an online shop with Nike, but the fact that the only place a link can be placed is in the bio/header of an account is not a good thing. The biggest issue with social media is,

Social Media is not indexed.

I isolated this sentence because even the biggest sneaker company in the world understands that social is a part of the entire package, but creating pages indexed via Webmaster Tools (Bing and Google) is a more powerful tool long term as search is much more important than social in web traffic. Remember the majority of the sneaker buying world doesn't engage in sneaker culture. They buy shoes for a specific reason, just as much as they do for fashion. Search is no longer Google dominated as it relates to products. It is more important than ever to create sites that are indexed by the two biggest search engines, Google and Bing, because Amazon is also shaping retail via search. In a post in 2017 I wrote the following words[44],

> What Amazon understands is that the majority of holiday shopping will be done via search and that apparel is a major item of purchase during the holidays. Both adidas and Under Armour should be paying very close attention to this introduction of sportswear by Amazon... specifically in Men's. Women's brands

[44] https://arch-usa.com/adidas-and-under-armour-amazon-has-arrived-source-12/

> should also find reason to worry as the majority of items purchased in women's sportswear isn't brand specific.

The above quote was in regard to brands overlooking Amazon Private Label and how Amazon has the ability to control the way consumers shop because they have created their own brands to compete against Nike and the other footwear and apparel companies. If a customer is beginning a search on Amazon then brands and retailers have to worry. The e-commerce giant is a destination site for browsing when people are looking for any product. Amazon understands this and they have utilized their data to create opportunities for their business.

Search is a considerable amount of web traffic and Amazon now rivals Google for search; in 2016 Power Reviews noted that, "A survey of 1,000 US consumers conducted by Power Reviews found that Amazon is the preferred starting point for product search. Google comes in a close second, followed by brand/retailer sites and e-commerce marketplaces (eBay, Etsy, etc.):

Amazon — 38 percent

Google — 35 percent

Brand or Retailer Site — 21 percent

Other eCommerce Marketplaces — 6 percent"

Combining brand and retailer is a mistake. As I mentioned earlier Nike dominates sneaker online search and website traffic. Retailers are competing *against* brands. They can no longer be grouped together. In 2016 sneaker retail didn't have the numerous third party shopping options that are available in 2018. This means that "other eCommerce Marketplaces" in the sneaker industry today has to include Grailed, GOAT, StockX, Poshmark and sites owned by sneaker lifestyle websites.

Amazon exists at the top because they continue to change the game. In 2018 the battle for search dominance shifted to voice via Alexa and Google Home, which further limits the reach of retail sites and creates more competition. In the short term, small retailers of footwear, specifically urban retailers, have a clear advantage in their core customer who is cash based. This is no longer a moat for urban retail as PayPal.me, Venmo, and Cash App have empowered the unbanked cash customer. Amazon is also considering a move to open store locations which would allow for Amazon to implement drop off location/ *pickups* for customers new to digital shopping who might not live in areas conducive to delivery options. If Amazon begins to open Whole Foods, or stores in food deserts, this can speed up the process of Amazon reaching the unbanked consumer with a drop off location in Whole Foods. I know this is purely speculative, but the iPod began with the thought of placing 1000 songs into your pocket. Retailers should be having this conversation.

Small Retailers can continue moving forward utilizing Google AdWords, paying influencers, and using social media ads. This would be par for the course. They would be doing what has always been done in marketing while Nike has launched a full strategic campaign that encompasses a social aspect, mobile applications, and Nike News (a CMS) and air.jordan.com (A CMS) as well as SNKRS (mobile App and CMS).

Doing what has always been done is shortsighted especially when Amazon and third party is an issue. Now consider this:

Barney's New York created The Window

http://thewindow.barneys.com/

Macy's created The Edit

https://www.macys.com/social/the-edit/

These are examples of established businesses utilizing CMS to drive engagement and long-form content to connect to their audience. I've mentioned Nike's SNKRS and Nike News, but here are the CMS sites of other brands carried in sneaker retail:

New Balance created *The Press Box*

https://newbalance.newsmarket.com/

Adidas created two distinct sites *GamePlanA* an interactive CMS launched about a year ago. https://www.gameplan-a.com/ and they also created *adidas News Stream* https://news.adidas.com/US

ASICS has 6 CMS based sites including a magazine: https://www.onitsukatigermagazine.com/?lang=en

I could continue to list the CMS sites for brands as well as large retailers, but I can't do the same thing for websites of Sneaker Retailers. This is a business issue that isn't relegated to footwear and apparel companies. Most businesses either don't have a CMS for their sites or they severely underutilize their CMS.

Companies are tied to Facebook and Google which require ads to drive engagement which means that they remain in a race to win keyword battles. That's a battle that can and will always be won by the company with the most money. Creative content however can allow a startup shoe company with one shoe style to become worth a billion dollars, see Allbirds[45]. Allbirds doesn't utilize a CMS, but their website is informative and provides the history and the technology that the brand uses in its simplistic sneakers. Now to be honest I see Allbirds encountering a moment where the brand will sell the technology they are using to create their eco-friendly footwear. Right now Allbirds doesn't need a CMS because unlike most brands/retailers

[45] Allbirds launched in 2014 with a Kickstarter. The name of the company at the time was Three over Seven. The Kickstarter funded at over 100,000 dollars in 24 hours. The company was built on one silhouette the wool runner shoe. After moving to Silicon Valley the company has now been valued at a billion dollars. All on the strength of their direct to consumer strategy.

their business is built on sustainability. Having a mission resonates with potential customers.

Allbirds is telling the story of creating footwear that is good for the environment. Their brand is their content. I haven't said this explicitly, but when a company or brand has storytelling built into its DNA this is equivalent to creating daily content when there is only a single product being pitched. Allbirds until recently only had one shoe that they made. Retailers have a thousand stories to tell about every brand they carry. Think about that last sentence.

When I began to adjust the strategy for the ARCH site to be more content driven in 2015, I created AHN and it took another year to really understand my new direction. I eventually wrote a business plan in October of 2016. Since that time the network has seen an increase in both Ad Revenue and Affiliate Revenue as well as followers.

To experiment with how effective ARCH was in driving traffic to other sites I removed the Adsense html codes and replaced them with brand relationships. In the last year AHN worked with three different brands, Ewing Athletics and OdorKlenz. The third campaign to test how content could drive traffic, I worked with 3DShoes to help build their CMS and blog which led to a book being written by a Benzinga journalist on the potential of the 3D footwear industry. These relationships were short term. I had never charged a company to create a campaign prior to Ewing Athletics. I had to learn how to set fees and create html ads for the products that Ewing Athletics wanted to be featured on the site. The campaigns were not lucrative, but they were very informative.

I took on the responsibility of creating the leaderboard, skyscraper and square ads to place in the header and sidebars. I then had to create the html code and make it adjust for mobile browsing. This was trial and error because writing code is not my strongest skill. I'm stating this for the person who has been thinking about starting a business as an ad company. I taught myself to write code and was paid for the work although I had never created a campaign before (outside of what I did for my own companies).

I had to keep track of all exit links via several analytic programs like Statcounter and of course Google Analytics. I had to rotate ads to keep the links fresh. The experience taught me a lot about offering advertising services. I have not pursued new dedicated ad relationships with any other brands as the goal for me has always been to research the significance of long-form content in creating exit link traffic and engagement. I also wanted to better understand just why multi-million dollar websites like Complex, Highsnobiety, and Hypebeast were able to get to the valuations they have. The campaign with Ewing Athletics ran on both Housakicks.com and arch-usa.com. I'm including the report that was sent to David Goldberg (CEO of Ewing Athletics) when the campaign was complete:

> Thanks for working with AHN from September 20th, 2017 through October 4th, 2017.
>
> During your campaign we created several posts pointing to your Ewing Athletics website in addition to creating the ads featured on the site in the header and sidebar. Below are breakdowns of the visits to the posts and a breakdown of exits from the sites. You will notice that the engagement on posts is much better. This shows that content drives engagement more than static ads. The exit links are in Excel CSV format and they are attached in a zipped folder. The information shows all exits from the site including exits to Ewing.

We are including all of the exits to give you an idea of what information and locations people are leaving AHN via links in articles and through affiliate links and article links. While we deleted all Google Adsense from the desktop, both sites have Google Ads enabled on Mobile. This is why there are some Google Ads shown in the exit links.

Observations

Our observation of the Ewing site is that it needs to be updated and a blog featuring the same information you share via Social Media should be added to the site to increase traffic. While I know that Ewing is a small brand, your interaction on Social needs to be increased and whenever possible you should answer questions and be as engaging as possible to increase potential conversions. I know that you are limited on what you can write about, but for every release your blog/site should deliver about 5 posts on each shoe style and a video of the photo shoot for additional marketing via YouTube.

You should refrain from sharing pictures of footwear without having splash pages for a click through or pre-order. If you don't have pages setup on the site when sharing pictures, then always place a link to the Ewing site. I think with a better site your engagement and conversion would skyrocket. These are just observations and not a part of your ad purchase on AHN.

The last two pages of this report are the links for both ARCH and Housakicks showing you the visits to Ewing articles.

Combined Views on AHN: **1,125 combined views** (These Views can be considered click through rates. They are stories about the brand, not page views. Page Views are below. The best thing about this is these articles are there forever so the value of your ad purchase lasts beyond these two weeks. 8 of your shoes have also been added to the ARCH Online Shop)

Daily Visits to Ewing Athletic Posts on AHN: **80.36 combined Visits per day**

Exits from the AHN to Ewing Athletics: **56 (CTR of 4.98%)**

Daily Visits to Ewing from AHN: **4**

Number of Impressions via ARCH: **10,538 Visits (Google Analytics 4,444 Page views)** these are impressions that help with branding. Every time someone visited the site they encountered Ewing Branding

Number of Impressions via Housakicks: **30,169 Visits (Google Analytics 12,485 Page views)**

Total Number of Impressions on AHN: **40,707 Visits (Google Analytics 16,929 Page views)**

I have to stress that this was the first time I set up a marketing campaign for a brand to work with AHN. The information allowed me to realize that if Ewing Athletics developed a better site that included content, the traffic generated would derive from a native source. Since this campaign the brand has improved their website layout and added staff to better respond on social and to actively market via e-mail. They haven't created a CMS, but Ewing isn't a heavily staffed company so the work they have done is solid. Their campaign with AHN is still paying off as the content written about the brand on the AHN is still sending traffic to the Ewing site. That's the benefit of content that can be indexed.

Blogs are no longer sites where people are sharing their ideas as a hobby. Blogs/Content Management Systems have parlayed content into investments and the blogs are monetizing through ad revenue, affiliate revenue and e-commerce. The blog has become a disruptive force in the sneaker industry. The blog has allowed *small* to shape a new consumer experience.

Take Highsnobiety as an example. Earlier this year, "Felix Capital[46] invested 8 Million dollars into the lifestyle blog." This investment is allowing Highsnobiety to make e-commerce 30% of the company's revenue. In my article on this investment I discussed,

> When a site begins to garner considerable traffic brands will pay for those eyes on that site. Complex became a media company with video and long-form content at the core of its business model. Highsnobie-

46 https://arch-usa.com/when-a-blog-garners-an-investment-a-decision-must-be-made-highsnobiety-e-commerce/

ty's recent investment demanded that the content company become something more.

Solecollector, under Complex, launched Slang

Campless became StockX

Kicks on Fire has Kixify

Hypebeast added HBX

Blogs/media companies have to find a way to diversify their income. The launch of private collections and an e-commerce platform by Highsnobiety is a natural addition that will be a case study in the integration of content into commerce, and commerce into content.

When I make the claim that traditional retail is under fire from e-commerce, when it comes to a digital platform like GOAT it becomes apparent that the disruption can quickly move from online into the physical world. GOAT, originally just a digital resale app, acquired Flight Club, the brick and mortar resale shop. The acquisition is going to create more locations for Flight Club across the U.S. GOAT opened a pop-up Flight Club location in Miami recently. I have to assume that this location, planned for six months, will continue to operate after acquiring the data from the pop-up. At any point an addition to the already crowded retail sneaker market is a disruption.

As I was editing this book, Foot Locker made a 100 Million dollar investment into GOAT Group. While many news articles see this as Foot Locker making an acquisition to get better, I believe Foot Locker recognized the threat GOAT presented and invested to prevent GOAT's expansion into brick and mortar. Which really shows the seriousness of Nike's play.

When Nike's CDO is taken into consideration the entire sneaker business becomes more complex.

Traditional retail is at a crossroads. Stores can double down on customer service and customer experience as well as improving their digital platform, but this is not the same sneaker environment it was ten years ago. With the rise of investments into sneaker blogs and third party resale platforms, traditional retail has to continue to evolve.

AHN is a startup lifestyle/business sneaker blog that has seen considerable growth. With 10,000 unique visits per month and websites catering to both sneakerhead culture and the business elements of sneaker culture, we have grown 6000% since our official launch in

October 2016. AHN garners over 6 page views per visit. 83% of the network's traffic is generated by organic search. This means that we do not rely on the inconsistency of social media. Our visitors either find our site arriving via search, or by visiting from direct links (12%). AHN consists of two people… 2.

AHN's growth is evidence that retailers could use to reverse engineer the entire ecosystem driving investment into digital e-commerce sneaker retail. Companies need media/content creation divisions which will drive daily engagement with their brand and website.

If AHN is currently earning over 700,000 dollars via third party sneaker sales, and 10,000 unique monthly visits (150,000 page views a month) there is a clear disconnect from consumer to retailer. If retail outlets were doing what we are doing, AHN wouldn't exist because I would probably be working for a chain as a writer. Instead AHN has grown as a two person team although Tayib and I don't have the ability to work full time on the sites. Imagine what could be possible for retailers who begin to utilize long-form content in their marketing plans with marketing divisions already in place.

Nike isn't slowing down their CDO. They plan on owning 80% of their distribution in North America by 2020. Retailers carrying the brand are already seeing how the company is aligning with particular retail outlets. What isn't being considered is if Nike continues to increase their growth in e-commerce how they will begin to limit what they send to their wholesale accounts? Amazon's Brand Registry and Private Label are continuing to be overlooked, and becoming stronger while continuing to cut into the e-commerce growth of smaller chains.

Retailers have to create a new system by adding in-house media teams delivering branding and *clicks through* to their own platforms. Surviving Nike's CDO, or surviving every brand's *Direct to Consumer* strategy, is the most important point of discussion that should be taking place by businesses operating on wholesale relationships. Those who begin to look at this seriously will be ahead of the curve.

Chapter 19

The Importance of Long-Form Content

I know this has been a long problem and solution discussion and I haven't discussed the year I spent on StockX, but this is one of the more complex books I've written for a number of reasons. There are a lot of articles and books on the benefits of *direct to consumer*. That information explains in great detail the benefits of offering products to your customer without a middleman. I've attempted to find information on the results of what happens when a brand that traditionally wholesaled its product switches gears and implements a DTC strategy. There hasn't been a real analysis of this effect. In footwear there have only been reports on the footwear industry based on point of sales data from previous quarters. I've been researching Nike's

Consumer Direct Offense for about four years. It only had the CDO name since late 2017.

In 2017 the data showed that adidas had passed Jordan Brand to become the number two footwear company in the U.S[47]. Sneaker blogs and business websites wrote stories to talk about this comeback for adidas. I didn't readily accept the data. Instead I took into consideration that the point of sales data derived from major retailer's credit card transactions and did not include Nike's doors and sales channels. I took the time to write an analysis using a logical approach based on the growth Nike showed in consecutive years:

Nike's direct-to-consumer sales grew in this manner:

2014 (768 Nike stores)

2015 DTC 6.6 Billion (832 Stores)

2016 DTC 7.9 Billion (919 Stores)

2017 DTC Revenue 9.1 Billion (985 Stores)

---

[47] https://arch-usa.com/why-you-should-question-npds-data-about-adidas-overtaking-jordan-brand/

I don't know the source of the data used to show adidas' ascent. What I do know is that Nike grew the number of their physical stores from 919 to 985 stores since 2016. THIS IS IMPORTANT: I don't need to know the source data to understand that as Nike grew e-commerce and in store sales via Nike Factory, Nike Clearance and Nike Employee Stores, that the natural progression for Nike footwear at retail would be a decrease in sales.

Did adidas take shares of the retail market from Nike?

YES

Did Nike lose money overall last year to this year? NO

A few FACTS from Nike's last quarterly report:

• Fourth quarter revenues up 5 percent to $8.7 billion; 7 percent growth on a currency-neutral basis*
• Fiscal 2017 revenues up 6 percent to $34.4 billion; 8

> percent growth on a currency-neutral basis*
> • Inventories up 4 percent as of May 31, 2017
>
> Pay close attention to the growth of Nike at the time that adidas "jumped" over the Jumpman. Nike's growth arrived from global sales and DTC primarily. The picture isn't clear on whether adidas really surpassed Nike when Nike's DTC is taken into consideration. Although I am not privy to the data from the company providing the information on sales positions of sneaker companies, when you consider that Nike grew their revenue 1.2 Billion from 2016 Q4 to 2017 Q4 on the strength of DTC there is more to the story of growth.

The information in the quote above provided a look at how DTC shaped the market, but it didn't speak to how sales at large retail chains and small retail chains were affected.

The reports that provide journalists with information on the top selling shoes and brands arrive at the end of each quarter. The data tells the readers what happened in a previous quarter or in the last year in an attempt to predict what could happen in the future. The problem in footwear is the momentum and hype around a brand shifts far too quickly to measure where companies are going in the next year based on information from the previous year.

Champion, Vans and Fila saw considerable growth in 2018. The point of sales data from 2017 would have never told you that these three brands would bounce back into prominence in 2018. What could have told someone on Wall Street that Champion was going to bounce back would have been if data from third party and resale would have been taken into consideration. During 2018 because AHN began an experiment in resale we noticed that the Fila Disruptor at the end of 2017 heading into 2018 was becoming a shoe that garnered a resale value. This information was available because Tayib decided to list the shoes on eBay above retail on a whim. When he sold 30 pair he contacted me to see if I had any luck with them. This moves me too far ahead. What I'm explaining here is that the data from previous quarters would not have given us any indication that Fila had turned a corner.

Since there aren't any reports that show how DTC shapes Nike's wholesale accounts I want to take a quick look at Nike's Q1 2019 and look at a wholesale account for Nike from the same quarter. Nike's Fiscal year starts in July to September. I'm not using Foot Locker because Foot Locker's growth for years has always been in line with Nike's growth. Hibbett Sports is on a traditional quarter system so Nike's Q1 would sync with their Q3.

- Nike North America, recorded a 6% sales growth in Q1 2019
- Hibbett Sports total net sales decreased $20.9 million, negative 8.8% to $216.9 million compared with $237.8 million for the 13-week period ended October 28, 2017.

This is only one example, but I'm sure every store that relies on the Nike wall has been flat or has shown a small amount of growth as Nike continues to develop their CDO.

I've been dropping hints about the yearlong experiment that Tayib and I did on third party. Our year on our respective sales platforms provided considerable input on how hot brands were. Tayib's year in resale on eBay and on Housakicks in Quarter 4 of 2017, heading into Quarter 1 of 2018 provided considerable evidence of Fila's sneaker the Disruptor selling above retail.

It's important for me to finish up why retailers and brands both should be laser focused on content.

Nike's Consumer Direct Offense strategy has placed retailers who carry the brand in a precarious position. For the first time in history brick and mortar accounts carrying Nike aren't simply battling other stores for consumers, they have to take on the brand itself as Nike looks to control 80% of the inventory they deliver to consumers in North America. During the introduction of CDO the brand stated they would cut down their relationships with retailers from 30,000 to 40. This is not an unheard of strategy. Startups that have launched in this era of social media have cut out the middleman to amazing success.

Direct-to-consumer is no longer the realm of door to door salesmen. Social media has empowered brands and given companies a straight line to the customer. Marketing has changed with the rise of social media and digitally native companies. The companies that were born on the internet like Warby Parker understood the importance of an active website. Unfortunately many established businesses, and many startups, have foregone their own websites and platforms to try and capture customers where they are; on the various social platforms. Nike however has added *long form content* as a component to their strategy to considerable benefit.

This book is a call to arms for any person or company attempting to navigate the shifting landscape of business marketing. Social media has completely changed the way brands reach the people who are loyal to their products. As more brands begin to function like e-commerce startups with direct-to-consumer tactics, instead of relying solely on the traditional retail/wholesale format, retailers have to consider the importance of their marketing strategies. Relying solely on Google Adwords, Facebook Ads and Influencer Marketing campaigns without developing the retail/brand website is a mistake.

Search engines remain a critically important aspect of marketing. As Amazon and Google begin to ramp up tactics to move consumers to their own business sites, a static website is no longer an effective tool for attracting new customers. Retailers can no longer add a product and wait on the consumer. Retailers and brands have to build sites and utilize long-form content that will be indexed and searchable. If the brand is doing this, then the retailer, small business person, entrepreneur has to do the same.

The sneaker industry is built on the back of irrational behavior. If a person has a pair of shoes for work and a pair of shoes for extracurricular activities that is all a person really needs. This is why the stories in footwear are important. It's why Jesse Owens being given a pair of track spikes by Adi Dassler is a cornerstone of the foundation of the Three Stripes. It's why the death of a blonde haired distance runner created the foundation of the Swoosh. It's why the story of the NBA banning a red, black and white shoe is the foundation of signature footwear.

There has to be something that connects the desire of people to be a part of a greater moment or event for them to purchase sneakers;

because buying more than one pair of shoes is an irrational decision based on wants. As soon as the consumer realizes that they don't need to have the latest model then the boom in sportswear will end. One of the only things that can keep the machine moving is the story: informative, emotional, educational, entertaining, stories delivered on a daily basis.

Chapter

20

e-Commerce: Sneaker's Last Growth Area

Throughout this book I discussed third party marketplaces. The third party has long been considered as inconsequential especially as it relates to the "reselling" of sneakers. This can't be argued typically because there has never been a real data set delivered to justify or explain how important resale is to the entire sneaker ecosystem. Actually there has been a data set utilized. It came from the website Campless.com. I explained that Campless became StockX, but why is that important and what proof is there that the rise of StockX is symbolic of an issue in the footwear industry that can be compared to issues in other businesses? To get to this discussion a bit of background has to be delivered.

I spent the entire year of 2018 selling on one platform. That platform was StockX. In 2017 I tested the marketplace on a very limited basis. I only sold 85 pair of shoes for a total of 14,500 dollars. That's an average price of 170.00 per pair. Had I made an analysis of the platform based on my limited time there I would have stated that StockX would never be an issue for retailers. The company existed in 2017 as a place where sneakers sold at the premium end of the footwear spectrum.

The majority of sales in the footwear business, as a company like Hibbett Sports stated in a recent conference call, are in the 60 dollar range per transaction. This is why Hibbett Sports acquired City Gear in 2018[48]. The premium range of footwear offers a few obvious things, bigger margins and a customer that purchases more than one sixty dollar shoe per year. One *sneakerhead* adds more value to a store than one traditional customer, but there are more traditional shoppers available.

This makes for an interesting internal battle taking place in sneaker retail. Big Box stores like Dick's and Academy cater to tradi-

---

[48] Hibbett Sports acquires City Gear Conference Call

tional shoppers. Marshalls, Kohl's and Ross also cater to the traditional customer. Foot Locker and Finish Line cater to both and stores like Shoe Palace and Jimmy Jazz cater to the premium buyer. Every customer is important, but if a company wants to reach every segment a line has to be straddled. Foot Locker is the only retailer that straddles the line successfully. Which is why when the market shifts Foot Locker is capable of adjusting to cater to the latest trend. Other footwear retailers have had to merger. It's a logical solution to straddling the line.

Hibbett Sports acquired City Gear and its 100 plus stores. City Gear's transactions are at 90 dollars per. 100 City Gear stores with a weak e-commerce division is equal to 200 Hibbett Sports and since Hibbett Sports recently corrected a major problem (e-commerce) that was moving the company towards a cliff, this acquisition could have serious upside.

Acquisitions in the sneaker world will continue because Nike is pushing their wholesale accounts to the limit. DTLR and Villa merged, but smaller chains like DTLR/Villa will probably be absorbed into bigger footwear retailers. Finishline was acquired by JD Sports; which wasn't a matter of mainstream and urban merging. The JD Sports acquisition was an international play by JD Sports entering the largest market in the world in North America. A company like the smaller Eblens chain was recently acquired by J.W. Childs Associates; but it will still either have to adjust or be assimilated (I'm an old school Trekkie and anytime I can use the Borg as a reference I do it).

The City Gear acquisition was required for a large chain like Hibbett Sports to capture premium sales as that area continues to grow while the low end at sneaker retail is flat. I contend that there are more sneakerheads being born every day because sneaker culture is now *mainstream*. However, the acquisitions taking place aren't just a case of businesses looking to enter *urban* retail; in this instance urban is synonymous with premium. Premium is where all of the investment and innovation in the sneaker industry is taking place. Innovation is where growth is incubated. The acquisitions are out of necessity.

Nike's Consumer Direct Offense is the primary culprit, but Nike can't be held solely responsible for the shift at retail. Self-inflicted, poor decisions around online e-commerce by small retail chains are just as responsible. Eblens has over 50 stores and the business doesn't have an e-commerce platform. The issues with direct to consumer and e-commerce are considerable problems, but both retailers and brands aren't taking advantage of Nike's aggressiveness in expanding their own doors. What do I mean by this? As Nike looks to reach its consumer there is considerable opportunity for new footwear brands and established footwear brands to amp up their relationships with retailers. The locations are already there, they don't have to open new doors, they only have to merchandise the stores better and build stores inside of stores.

Other brands should see Nike shifting to this 80/20 strategy as an opportunity. Over the course of 2018 however I haven't seen any increased marketing or product development by brands, and retailers have continued using old merchandising and store layouts without any new in-store concepts to drive foot traffic. Nike is moving and everyone else seems stuck. Actually Hibbett Sports isn't stuck and neither are third party sites like StockX and GOAT, but I want to discuss quickly why Hibbett Sports holds the key to proving the power of e-commerce.

A few years ago I wrote an article about Hibbett Sports and I made a claim that the chain would become the next Sports Authority and go bankrupt. The article was in response to the lack of analysis around Hibbett's 14% stock price drop:

> Hibbett Sports has been considering moving westward. They just opened their first store in California. In the article I wrote last year I explained that the logistics would prove to be a nightmare for the southern based company and that instead of focusing on expanding the company westward, capital would be better allocated in redesigning the stores and improving their e-commerce, customer experience and merchandising.
>
> I said that the expansion would increase expenses, decreasing margins and drive the share price down once reports became available. I said mid 30s… It was worse than that as the shares now sit at 30.15 and when you enter any Hibbett Sports they still have the same very evident problems with merchandising and they have yet to figure out their e-commerce strategy.
>
> Instead of repairing their customer loyalty program in house they hired a team from Baesman Insights:

> http://www.nasdaq.com/press-release/baesman-insights–marketing-scores-new-partnership-with-hibbett-sports-inc-20170214-01044
>
> While this is commendable, a repairing of customer loyalty programs is not the primary issue. What is the issue?
>
> e-commerce – When the brands you carry are generating amazing content and making it available via the web in multiple locations including their websites because they understand the importance of connecting with this generation's consumer is based on more than just product, shouldn't you be taking notice? Hibbett Sports has not. Instead of expanding west, they could have taken that money, built a content creation and social media team, redesigned their horrible website and instantly reaped the benefits of engagement with their prospective audience.

That quote above could have been written about any small retailer. Hibbett Sports isn't small. They have over 1000 stores. While I still think the expansion into the West will become an issue, because Hibbett Sports actually did something that corrected their biggest issue they saved their company. Not long after I wrote the article above Hibbett Sports launched one of the best new websites in sneaker retail. Here is what I wrote about this move:

> When I wrote the article (mentioned above) and connected it to older posts I thought that Hibbett Sports

would be fading away. Since I wrote (the post in February 2017) I've been visiting stores and I've noticed that the line of sight from the register to the front door has improved as Hibbett Sports has taken to redesigning their store interiors. I stated this was important because of Loss Prevention issues. The company still has a lot of merchandise in each location, but all stores have this issue as retail is struggling to bring in buyers. The company has obviously begun to take merchandising more serious and it is showing.

My other complaint was about the expansion to the West Coast. I thought it was a mistake and I still do. I said that the best thing Hibbett Sports could do was launch an ecommerce platform. As one of the larger chains in the country, they didn't have an online shopping platform, until now.

In one of the best updates I've seen, the company launched their e-commerce platform and in staying on trend the site features on the front page the hottest brand in the world, adidas and the second hottest brand, Puma. Nike doesn't even make the front page of this updated version of the website which is a far cry from one of my biggest worries about Hibbett Sports, their reliance on Nike inventory.

The user interface on the site is clean and simple. I haven't purchased anything to see how quickly the company processes their orders, but if the market is paying attention this is a reason for them to get excited. It might be too late as Amazon begins to solidify its relationships with the Big Three through brand registries, and Foot Locker really dominates the landscape for online purchasing with brick and mortar sportswear stores, but this is a solid move by Hibbett Sports.

Hibbett Sports invested in their website. It doesn't have a CMS, but what they have done is integrate their online and brick and mortar in a seamless manner. They are using a system that allows for the site to pull from in-store inventory and the site features fantastic imagery with functional blocks of information on the homepage. The product listings are clear and the search is simple and effective. Hibbett Sports' website is ten times as good as Foot Locker's website and Foot Locker has more experience at online than the smaller Hibbett Sports. Hibbett's e-commerce is enough to possibly lift City Gear, but there are issues with City Gear that could hinder the merger and hurt Hibbett Sports, but that's for another discussion.

An effective online strategy is vital to continued growth for all businesses. Third Party Retail lives in this space. It was born here and of all of the platforms to arrive on the scene and of all of the established platforms, StockX has the most potential for disrupting the market. But… what exactly is StockX and how does it work? If I think the site is the most effective third party platform why isn't it considered a threat? I want to switch gears and take a closer look at StockX, but I can't move away from the discussion on brick and mortar without taking a moment to include observations of retail that can improve physical locations. An improvement of strategy in traditional stores holds valuable opportunity for e-commerce growth as well. There is also an opportunity for stores to market across segments of the population vs building brick and mortar to attract only millennials.

Chapter 21

How Can Sneaker Retail Adjust?

This section is based on sneaker retail, but honestly everything being written here applies to almost any business adjusting to the growth of e-commerce. Grocery Stores are adjusting to the Whole Foods acquisition by offering services like Clicklist at Kroger and Curbside for Wal-Mart. Tech Stores like Best Buy have had to adjust to brands and retail chains offering free shipping on products.

There is even disruption in the furniture market with IKEA and *do it yourself.* Macy's understood that they had to offer something extra to regain their share of the furniture market so they created *White Glove installation* which gives the buyer free delivery and set-up for bedroom sets and other large furniture items. Every business has had to make some adjustment to the digital landscape. Smaller retail chains as I've said throughout this book, are encountering issues that they've never had to deal with in fighting back against the brands they carry. At brick and mortar locations there isn't much being done to offset this new challenge outside of promotion of sales.

Retailers have been in the promotional cycle for years which has contributed to *customer restraint.* Customers, in particular cash customers, are more patient than they have ever been in purchasing. As smaller chains move quickly towards discounting prices on products within two weeks in some instances on 'new releases', customers realize this. The impulse to buy on "release day" doesn't work as well as it once did in converting the consumer. This is also a problem created by Nike and their ability to reach the buyer via sneaker blogs and through their own apps and websites.

Sneaker retail has to make a decision to develop better shopping experiences because the traditional cash customer is now experiencing online retail. Uninformed sales leads, dismissive and confrontational store personnel can no longer get away with mistreating the consumer and still get those dollars. A better store has to be created.

Small Solutions for Brick and Mortar

I'm taking a moment to deviate from the primary purpose of this book to discuss some changes at brick and mortar stores. While this is not my forte I've visited countless stores and I felt the need to share a few ideas.

Music

Why is music important? In every sneaker retailer music is meant to build ambiance. Retail is entering a moment where both brands and stores are failing to realize that the generation that started this "sneakerhead" trend is actually middle aged now, but they are still shopping. The potential is there for stores to cater to dads and sons, mothers and daughters. This can be done by something as simple as a curated playlist featuring the Golden Era of Hip-Hop and the modern era.

I discussed the rise in older shoppers in an article called *The Shifting Demographics of Sneakerheads*[49]. In this article I shared a post from a visitor to the site,

> Even though I'm just entering my 40s, I just cop'd my favorite pair of kicks for the first time… the Air Jordan 3. When I first seen the Tinkers on the SNKRS app, with it coming to fruition the way originally intended, I knew I had to have them. 4/30 7a came, and I had the app ready to get a special pair of my favorite kicks since they first came out when I was a young'n. Coming Soon to Buy $200 @ 7a I clicked buy and got in the queue. Only doing that once before w the Vintage Box AF270s and getting them. Heart racing, waiting, finally said "Sorry out of stock." Crushed. But determination kicked in and I found a pair in 13s for $260. Got'm yesterday. 😎 Smell was strong , fingernail polishy, and felt good to finally have a pair of 3s, and a special edition pair at that. Now I'm torn be-

[49] https://arch-usa.com/the-shifting-demographics-of-sneakerhead-culture/

tween wearing them or not. LOL My bad, just wanted to share.

Catering to the OG sneakerhead crowd and the young crowd is an advantage for all of retail, but read that paragraph again and note the price of the shoes. The buyer first went to Nike's website to purchase but missed out. The shoe was the Air Jordan 3 Tinker. The model retailed for $200.00. With tax the shoes should have cost around 217.00. The visitor to my site named Mike, went on to explain that when he found the shoes had sold out on Nike, he didn't go to Foot Locker or Finish Line, he went to StockX; hence the price of $260.00 dollars. I can repeat constantly that the market has shifted. I've shown that StockX and other third party sites are visited at a rate comparable to brick and mortar, established businesses, I will get into this in a much deeper manner, but there is a problem when this happens with regularity. It may not have anything to do with brick and mortar, but if Mike had a local store that catered to him as well as catering to younger sneaker fans, he could have walked into Foot Locker and used the Stock Locator feature to order his shoes at retail pricing. I'm not saying music would have made this happen, but consider that for Mike this was an emotional connection to his youth. If he walked in and songs from OutKast's *Southernplayalistic* or Nas' *Illmatic* was playing instead of Lil Yachty and Lil' Baby playing over and over, the combination of music and product would have formed a bridge to purchase.

Update POS Systems

Another in-store advantage is implementing new POS and inventory systems. The loss prevention value of wall scanning systems for checking on shoes creates a great opportunity to give consumers a feeling that the store has nothing to hide. Many sneaker retailers have serious issues with staff hiding shoes that are popular. When a retail outlet has a chance to earn customer loyalty it can be severely fractured when the customer feels that a sales lead is lying about the inventory. More important is the reduction in stolen merchandise. Many stores are shorthanded. A tactic for many thieves is to arrive in groups and take advantage of the lack of employees manning the floor. Most loss prevention problems happen because a sales lead has to leave the floor to check sizes. With the cash registers in the back of most stores and at an angle where apparel can't be seen, snatch and grabs take place because older POS systems are slow and they don't allow customers to handle transactions where they stand.

Refining Retail

Retailers have an opportunity to further refine their businesses by creating levels for sales leads. Employees at shoe stores treat their jobs as temporary launch pads or paychecks. Retail stores see considerable turnover because the jobs are considered stepping stones. Young people come into a sneaker retailer with the idea that they cannot make their job into a career. There is not a clearly defined path to improvement, raises and promotion, provided by hardly any sneaker retail stores. Footlocker does a great job of explaining that a sales lead can become a keyholder, an assistant manager and potentially earn a manager's position. Also in their chain is the potential to become a buyer, auditor, DM or RVP.

While Foot Locker does a good job of establishing where an employee can grow, they do have an issue with the ceiling that managers encounter. I've seen some of the best young minds exit Foot

Locker stores because they realized that the store was their ceiling. Somewhere in sneaker retail there has to be more opportunity created. In smaller retail chains it appears that the treatment of employees at the lower level is a considerable issue. If I was asked what is the issue that will hurt sneaker retail the most in the near future, my answer would be without pausing, the lack of support for in-store staff and the failure to pay employees more. I understand that margins are poor in sneakers, but unfortunately the pay is not poor in the third party marketplace. Every store chain has a problem with employees now being aware of the value of the shoes they carry because of sites like StockX and GOAT. The treatment of employees and the pay in this new environment is the biggest issue at retail because the opportunities aren't clear. When there isn't any hope to either earn greater job satisfaction or money, sneaker companies create nihilists.

This lack of opportunity creates issues that manifest in loss prevention issues[50] and high turnover for part time workers and full time workers who simply do not see an opportunity for job growth.

---

[50] "Loss prevention" in this text at this point is referring to how store employees at sneaker stores are not willing to place the effort into being better employees because they simply don't see the end benefit. This inability to take the job serious leads to items being stolen from the store and other 'loss prevention' issues.

Stores that offer the chance to build a career with the company will find better employees and better work environments. This begins with the people at the bottom of the chain, Sales Leads. The Sales Lead job can be given more status and in turn produce better results for the company. One of the problems at retail stores is resale and managers attempting to *game* the system on "big release" days. This can be prevented when the people at the low end of the chain of command are empowered.

The introduction of levels for sales leads can be created to inspire commitment to the company. I've seen stores in my area in the last few months fire entire staffs from managers to sales leads at multiple locations. Loss prevention is an issue, employees utilizing discounts, and employees selling shoes to the highest bidder is a major problem. This is a problem at almost every sneaker store. If it is not a problem, customers feel that it is. On almost every retail dive that takes place on a 'major' release day there is the same narrative which can be overheard, "They're holding shoes for people."

This problem contributes to a lack of trust by customers with stores. It is my belief that the reason there are so many issues with loss prevention and customer loyalty at sneaker stores is because the guidelines to job promotion are not clearly defined and as I said earlier employees see their jobs as stepping stones or placeholders until something more 'serious' or better paying comes along. I think sneaker retail could improve if it implements something that I have pulled from my military background: Personnel Qualification Standards. PQS styled standards already are available in most stores in some form. However a more official booklet can be created, for sales leads, to create a stronger workforce at the lowest level, which in all honesty is the most important level.

The sales lead is the first person a customer encounters upon entering a store. If that employee feels that this is just a part time hustle, they will treat the job as such. This contributes to a poor customer experience. In today's retail environment where stores are facing challenges from the digital arena as well as other brick and mortar locations, the **customer experience is the most important thing to maintain growth for a company**. During retail dives one of the first noticeable things is that sales leads and managers often ignore the customer. There is very little enthusiasm and there is very limited product knowledge by sales leads. PQS combined with Sales Lead levels (presented below) can immediately change the look and feel of the workplace. Here is a list of the proficiency skills a sales lead should be evaluated upon:

- Sales leads should obviously be judged on these qualities: Appearance, Attitude, Performance, Attention to Detail, Merchandising, Inventory Control, Cashier's Duties, Depth of Product Knowledge and Punctuality
- Team members should learn Store Opening and Store Closing Routines. Shoe Cleaning Product Training (gloves should be provided by the store).
- Sales leads can be required to suggest information for Online Content. This is an example based on chains creating CMS for online promotion. A sales lead that submits suggestions will be aware of what is on the website and how they can engage the customer on the history of the product they are possibly going to pur-

chase. If stores include touch screen pads in-store programmed to feature the website posts on events and products, visitors will remember to leave the store and visit the website increasing transactions after a customer has left.

The reality is that very few sales leads stay with a company for longer than a year. If chains started a reward system for employees at the lowest level it would create loyalty. Reinforcing loyalty with a new rewards system can create a better customer experience because a happy employee enjoys opening the doors and the air of the entire store changes when the atmosphere is charged with positivity.

While this part of the book does not dig into how retailers can offset Nike's continued CDO growth, I felt that it was needed to establish that a new work environment caters to a stronger chain of command for the company. This is not my forte, but after doing retail dives and visits and looking at the turnover taking place at all sneaker stores and in retail, I felt that discussing this was important; on to StockX.

Chapter 22

Traditional 3rd Party is Already Disrupted

No one is looking at a company like StockX as a reason for issues with online growth in sneaker retail because once again… resale is inconsequential to a billion dollar industry; at least that's what executives and analysts think. StockX *is and can become* a major thorn in the side of Amazon and eBay and to be honest it already has become a thorn. The online platform is also a silent assassin striking brick and mortar locations, although StockX does not have a retail outlet. For those who haven't really heard of StockX, my quick definition of the app and website is that the site is Uber/AirBnB for sneaker e-commerce, with the potential to become much more. StockX does not warehouse the products sold on the channel. It acts as a thoroughfare, or a waystation for the products sold there.

In 2016 Campless, the sneaker site that collected data from eBay sales, transitioned into an app and online marketplace that would allow resellers and buyers the opportunity to buy sneakers inside of an ecosystem based on the most important aspect of acquiring rare and hard to find kicks, authenticity. StockX did not remain flat. The company shifted and expanded from sneakers to luxury handbags and into watches. The site also added Streetwear. From 2016 to 2018 the small startup added a location in Arizona and an international location[51] in the UK. Along the way in 2018 the company received a 44 Million dollar investment. In comparison the Hibbett Sports acquisition of City Gear was an 88 Million dollar cost. Think about it… StockX doesn't carry any inventory but just attained an investment of 44 Million half the value of a brick and mortar with over 100 stores, a Nike account and years of experience. StockX is two years old.

Throughout the book I've discussed why the disruptive segments of the sneaker industry have created a retail atmosphere unlike anything in the history of the business. Simply saying this amounts to hearsay. What is needed to nail down this conversation is data. There

---

[51] https://stockx.com/news/stockx-launches-in-europe/

are millions of dollars being left on the table in sneaker retail. This is money that either ingenious young people can capture as resellers or money that sneaker retail can begin to regain. It all depends on how this book is read.

When I began writing I mentioned several times that I spent all of 2018 on StockX solely as my resale platform of choice. This was important because it allowed me to discover every aspect of what makes StockX work. In any experiment there has to be a control and a variable. I stated my Amazon story because it established a baseline. I sold over 3 Million dollars in sneakers on Amazon. That is a baseline. I know that it's possible to make almost half a million per year as a one man company. I am the *control* working solely through StockX. I needed a *variable* so I asked my partner in AHN to spend the year selling on traditional resale platforms. Tayib sold on Amazon, eBay, Kixify, and on Housakicks.com. He started 2018 with inventory carried over from the previous year and he also picked up footwear from stores throughout the year. I began 2018 with 300.00 dollars and no shoes in inventory. As I've said several times throughout this book, the outcome of our experiment in 2018 shines an extremely bright light on the various issues with sneaker retail and the shift in sneaker e-commerce. Let's dive into the data via the *Variable*. In the Variable discussion my partner Tayib will present data based on his year of resale and he is comparing it to the CSV data I gave him from my year on StockX. Tayib is a college math instructor. His ability to crunch data is amazing. He can create formulas to find comparisons that are informative and educational. His analysis allows me to step away and provide a different point of view that doesn't derive from the work I've done. This is important because it establishes that the disruption to traditional third party resale is already here.

Chapter

23

Preface to the Resale Experiment

by Tayib Salami of Housakicks

Before I explain the contrast in sales for Chris (Control) vs my work (Variable) on traditional resale channels I need to deviate and dig into resale culture.

The most abhorred folks in the sneaker community are the hypebeasts and the resellers. The first group is hated simply because of their lack of originality and the second because of their capitalist nature. As much as resellers are scorned, they play an important role in the sneaker world for various reasons. Now that the sneaker game has gone mainstream, it has led to the birth of new third party market-places such as GOAT and StockX. The emergence of these platforms is causing havoc within the reseller's world by engendering what I call *vultures*: a new breed of resellers that have the potential to be very detrimental to the sneaker world. To shed more light on this new group, I will give a breakdown of the different types of resellers that exist within in our world (sneaker world I mean).

The Convenience Reseller:

These are probably the most compassionate resellers you'll ever come across. They resell for the love of the game, most are fellow sneakerheads that will go to a great extent to try to get their peers shoes they've been looking for. Their profit margin is not that significant (decent markup) and they basically are appreciated for looking out (or throwing alley oops) for other collectors. You'll usually find these guys in most social media sneaker groups. They almost operate like a 7/11, their profit margin like I said earlier isn't considered ridiculous hence they are tolerated or shall I say accepted.

The Dummy Reseller:

Folks in this category have zero clue what they are doing; they usually get up on any Saturday morning and hope to make a fortune on any Jordan retro (whether GR or limited) that Nike is releasing. Every now and then they may score a home run, but for the most part they foolishly invest their money into sneakers only to get stuck with them and suffer huge losses. They eventually give up the reselling game (and claim *reselling is dead* once they get burned a couple of times).

The Business Reseller:

Most of the guys in this group are also sneaker heads but with a lot of capital. They have figured out ways to turn their passion into a business. These are your typical eBay power sellers who have connections with sneaker boutiques, retailers and sometimes utilize shady tactics to acquire the gigantic inventory they have. Some are liked and others disliked, the latter because they are often viewed as spoiled brats that only have what they have because of daddy or mommy's money (some can be put in the hypebeast category). Many consignment stores fall under this category too but these are guys that have actually worked hard to get where they are (so no disrespect to them).

The Mathematician:

They are also sneaker heads who enjoy studying the shifting trends in the sneaker industry from a business standpoint. They can predict what shoes are going to do well in the retail market or third party marketplaces based on data they collect or past history. They resell because it's a hobby; some of them also do it because they have to pay the bills. They can be a great asset to brands, retailers and resellers that want to thrive in the industry.

The Vultures:

Guys in this category have zero interest in sneakers; they are in it for the money. Like biblical locusts, they destroy everything in their way and will stop at nothing to achieve their ends. A lot of them are bulk buyers from overseas who only buy certain sizes in kids and men's (size 3.5Y-6Y, size 7-9 in men's). They move silently and usually do not purchase with credit/debit cards (but cash money) and have people in every state. They move in waves into local malls/stores and buy out every size listed above. If you wonder why those sizes in certain styles are going for three times their retail price on eBay, StockX, or GOAT it's because they aren't available in stores anymore. This may sound like "hate" but it really isn't because there is a certain level of common courtesy that is lacking on their part. Yes everyone wants to make money, and I'm not against it but when it gets to the point where it's hurting other folks, then there's a problem. Most of them are shipping these sneakers overseas and in the process making it impossible for folks with smaller feet to get anything stateside. Everyone is affected by it and the ones suffering the most are the consumers. I'll give you an example that perfectly illustrates this problem:

Right now on StockX the *Air Jordan 1 Mid Hornets* reflects the absence of sizes 7 - 9.5 at retail locations throughout the country. The shoe retails at SRP $110.00.Sizes 7-9.5 on 1/19/2019 are selling for:

Size 7 - $244
Size 7.5 - $231
Size 8 - $229
Size 8.5 - $204
Size 9 - $206
Size 9.5 - $207

The larger sizes from 10 to 13 show a significant drop in price because these shoes are not coveted by the Vultures:

Size 10 - $167
Size 10.5 - $135
Size 11 - $100
Size 11.5 - $104
Size 12 - $88
Size 12.5 - $80
Size 13 - $87

The shoe released in April of 2018. Sizes are beginning to disappear from retail above size 9.5 so the Size 10 is reflecting this, which is natural when a shoe has been around for 8 months. The smaller sizes have been reselling at the markup since earlier this year. At retail the Hornets Mid 1 is now on sale in stores. The shoe is still available in stores in sizes 10.5 - 13 but not in sizes 9.5 and below. The bulk buyers completely ravaged every possible location within the USA and then sent them overseas (which speaks to the growth of sneaker culture internationally and why Nike and all brands are focused on China for future growth). The resale value is also happening with Grade School sizes as well. Particular models from size 3.5Y to size 5.5Y are selling out everywhere.

This information about the type of resellers there are is to show what type of sellers Chris and I represent. I'm the Mathematician. Chris is not a Mathematician, but on his site he used to write a feature called *Should You Buy to Flip?* Chris also taught a number of people who are now big resellers how to flip shoes. Chris has to be considered the Business Reseller.

Additional Information on Reselling by Chris

It's important to establish that retail is not fond of reselling. Brands are attempting to shut down bots. There are even government initiatives being legislated under an Anti-Bots bill[52]. Brick and Mortar locations are resorting to raffles via the apps, but these apps can't account for a shoe like the Air Jordan 1 Mid which originally wasn't a shoe that gained value in resale.

In all stores there are policies in place to prevent buyers from snatching every pair. Vultures understand this so this is why they move in groups and utilize cash because a cash purchase allows the store to do multiple transactions and groups can move around the policies that limit purchases. The problem occurs when these Vultures begin to utilize the tools stores like Footlocker put in place to build customer loyalty.

These Vultures will call and complete all of the surveys on the 30 receipts they get from transactions. These receipts are worth ten dollar discounts. Unfortunately for the store managers those surveys

[52] https://arch-usa.com/the-government-is-helping-sneakerheads-with-an-anti-bots-bill/

can hurt because the information that is collected is often rushed and doesn't truly reflect the store's service. The store is also hurt because previous year's sales are a measurement of growth for stores. When a store sees a spike in sales this can create a chain of events where the system can read a particular shoe as popular in a region. The system then allots a particular style to that store. This takes man hours and creates additional shipping costs for stores when they have to ship models to other stores.

When the Vultures complete their mission they disappear for weeks or months leaving stores without critical sizes in inventory which hinders the shoppers who are paid on schedule (every two weeks or every week) and may not be able to purchase a pair they want until a certain time of the month. While it seems that all resellers create this situation, this simply isn't the case. When a team/group of Vultures are in movement they can cover so much territory that in one day they can accomplish what a one person reseller would take weeks to months to do. While this sounds like crying over spilled milk, it isn't. When bulk buyers spend ten thousand dollars in one stop the store manager needs that money to hit goals and to keep the store running smoothly, but it completely disrupts the data the store uses.

The vultures will often kill the price of shoes which in turn forces stores to compete with unfair online prices. What do I mean by this? When a particular size sells out and isn't available stores are stuck with redundant sizes. This means that inventory sits and those new releases that should arrive at your favorite location, don't. The stores eventually have to mark down the remaining sizes. The third party marketplace reflects this lower price creating a chain reaction.

Vultures create situations where regular consumers are often penalized and can't use discounts or loyalty programs. Vultures create inventory issues that lead to stores not getting new drops. Vultures aren't for the culture.

Chapter 24

Control vs the Variable by Tayib Salami (founder of Housakicks)

I hope the previous section helped to give an understanding of how resale and the people who resale can be categorized. A couple of years ago, I wrote a post where I said that reselling was dead and couldn't be considered a legitimate business but more like a hustle.

Thou Shall Not Fool Thyself : Reselling Sneakers Isn't A Business[53]

Well, StockX is progressively changing the way I view reselling and this is my attempt to make my case. I was looking at my partner's sales data and was astonished with the number of transac-

[53] https://housakicks.com/uncategorized/thou-shall-not-fool-thyself-reselling-sneakers-isnt-business/

tions he was able to conduct as a one man operation for an entire year via StockX.

Below I've incorporated a portion of his CSV file to show you how many pairs this one man operation sold over 12 months[54].

4250	3730959	In Process	2018-12-30	LeBron 15 Black Bri	Nike-LeBron-15-Blac	AQ2363-002		10.5	$115.00
4251	3730984	In Process	2018-12-30	LeBron 15 Black Bri	Nike-LeBron-15-Blac	AQ2363-002		11	$105.00
4252	3734289	In Process	2018-12-30	adidas Deerupt Sola	Adidas-Deerupt-Sola	CQ2624		10	$51.00
4253	3734702	In Process	2018-12-30	Kyrie 4 Confetti	Nike-Kyrie-4-Confetti	943806-900/AJ1891		15	$218.00
4254	3734706	In Process	2018-12-30	Kyrie 4 Confetti	Nike-Kyrie-4-Confetti	943806-900/AJ1891		13.5	$210.00
4255	3734713	In Process	2018-12-30	Jordan 6 Rings White	Air-Jordan-6-Rings-W	322992-120		9.5	$100.00
4256	3734848	In Process	2018-12-30	adidas Stan Smith W	Adidas-Stan-Smith-V	M20324		9	$51.00
4257	3734850	In Process	2018-12-30	adidas POD-S3.1 Co	adidas-POD-S3-1-Co	B37366		10.5	$50.00
4258	3734851	In Process	2018-12-30	adidas NMD R1 Chal	adidas-NMD-R1-Chal	D96626		13	$51.00
4259	3734854	In Process	2018-12-30	adidas NMD R1 Chal	adidas-NMD-R1-Chal	D96626		8	$52.00
4260	3734858	In Process	2018-12-30	adidas NMD R1 Chal	adidas-NMD-R1-Chal	D96628		9.5	$50.00
4261	3734864	In Process	2018-12-30	adidas NMD R1 Core	adidas-NMD-R1-Core	D96627		10	$46.00
4262	3734887	In Process	2018-12-30	adidas NMD R1 Core	adidas-NMD-R1-Core	D96627		9	$55.00
4263	3735859	In Process	2018-12-31	Jordan 14 Retro Des	Air-Jordan-14-Retro-I	487471-021		8.5	$102.00
4264	3735864	In Process	2018-12-31	Jordan 14 Retro Des	Air-Jordan-14-Retro-I	487471-021		9	$101.00
4265	3739539	In Process	2018-12-31	Jordan 1 Retro High	Air-Jordan-1-Retro-Hi	555088-015		10	$176.00
4266	3739560	In Process	2018-12-31	Jordan 1 Retro High	Air-Jordan-1-Retro-Hi	555088-015		10	$176.00
4267	3739577	In Process	2018-12-31	Jordan 1 Retro High	Air-Jordan-1-Retro-Hi	555088-015		10	$175.00
4268	3740458	In Process	2018-12-31	Air More Uptempo W	Nike-Air-More-Uptem	415082-109	5.5Y		$95.00
4269	3740468	In Process	2018-12-31	Air Force 1 Low East	Nike-Air-Force-1-Low	AH8462-400		8	$114.00
4270 ⇦	3744479	In Process	2018-12-31	Air Max 97 Persian V	Nike-Air-Max-97-Pers	921826-103		10.5	$120.00

Chris sold over 4,200 pairs (4,270 pairs to be precise) in the course of 12 months while running a website, being a family man and doing other sneaker related activities. The question that came to my mind was: is reselling still dead? I looked at my own data and realized how terrible my sales were in 2018. It dawned on me - StockX has

[54] I actually sold 4,208 shoes during 2018. The StockX CSV includes pairs that were processed in January, but they were counted for December (note the words in process in the picture below). I did a video showing the inside of my dashboard with the correct numbers. You can find the video on my YouTube page. The numbers in this book will show 4,270.

redefined reselling. The individual with the right system in place has the potential to make a decent living with the platform.

StockX has become a game changer for someone that can take advantage of the fact that money has been left on the table by both brands and retail outlets. A reseller no longer has to cast a line and wait for the fish to come to the nets. StockX has changed the way re-sale takes place. Pictured is the dashboard from my eBay account. At one time I cherished my status with eBay with my life. I no longer fight as hard because I'm selling just as many shoes through my own site. While Chris sold more on StockX, the Housakicks side of the network sells more shoes directly to consumers than the ARCH-USA side of the network. I'm not presenting my website sales here because the Variable set was meant to research if reselling has shifted for third party platforms. Here are my sales on eBay:

Seller level (Region: US)	>
Current seller level	Below Standard
If we evaluated you today	Below Standard
Transaction defect rate	4.05%
Late shipment rate	9.01%
Tracking uploaded on time and validated	71.43%
Cases closed without seller resolution	1
Transactions (last 12 months)	247

I sold a total of 247 sneakers on eBay over the course of a year. I sold a total of 117 sneakers via Kixify over the course of 12 months. These are traditional locations for resale.

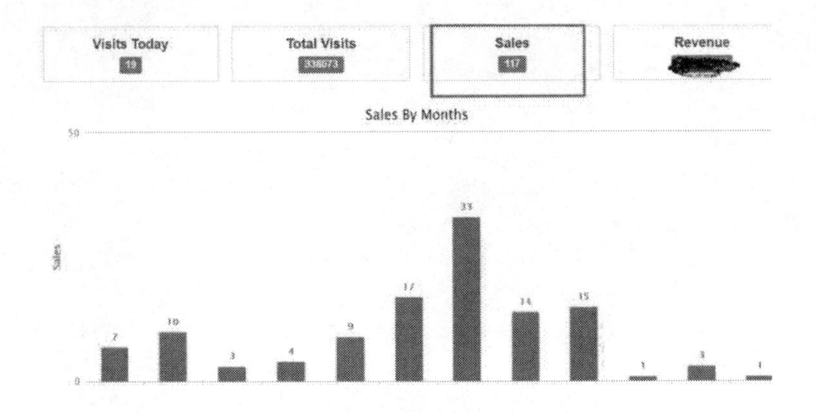

My sales on eBay and Kixify total up to 364 transactions against the 4270 achieved by my partner via StockX.

Let’s consider the 4270 pairs sold and run some numbers based on the worst case scenario for Chris.

- Chris’ minimum profit per pair was $10

- 4270 pairs in 12 months is the equivalent of selling 360 pairs a month or 12 pairs a day; here is the interesting part. Chris’ sales via StockX required no pictures to be taken, no descriptions to be added and no messages to be answered. All of the typical problems a seller can encounter on eBay or Kixify have been removed on StockX. StockX creates this situation: *I have the shoes and I’m willing to ac-*

cept the offer on them vs *I bought these shoes and I hope someone discovers it on eBay and pays me what I want.*

Acquiring 12 shoes a day for a Business Reseller is a walk in the park that may require a maximum of 4 hours a day (remember that Chris is running a sneaker news site as well). So for 4 hours, 12 shoes and a minimum profit of $10 per shoe, Chris possibly made a net profit of $42,700 on StockX within a year and that's the worst case scenario. I was very, very, very, very, conservative with the $10. Imagine how much more profit can be made on StockX with the right system in place.

Reselling is being restructured and those with a brain, a little bit of capital and 4 hours at their disposal can thrive in this new market. I put my partner's transactions next to mine and it was embarrassing.

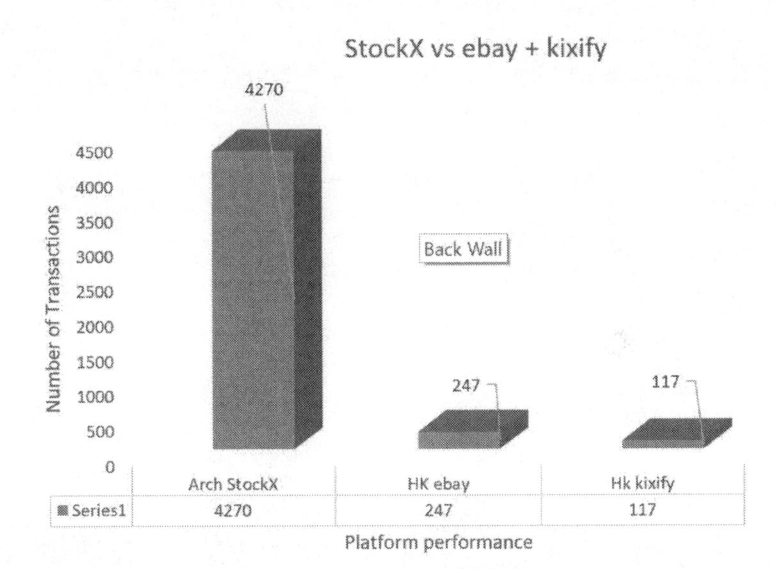

The only aspect that I can say makes my variable experiment the winner is that consistently writing content on the site, as well as placing the shoes I have for sale on my website, has resulted in my site generating sales. Chris did not do this because as the Control he didn't want to corrupt the data. This leads to another discussion since towards the end of the year as we completed our Variable and Control set I used Chris' model of resale and no longer purchased footwear outright. I am not carrying inventory anymore. I visit local stores and add the sizes I see to my site. The footwear selling through my site is from retail chains that have placed items on sale. I shouldn't be able to do what I'm doing and neither should Chris, but we both are active in resale. Retailers are leaving a lot of money on the table.

Chapter 25

StockX vs Amazon Part 1

Tayib's Variable set allows me to discuss my year on StockX with a bit of clarity. This information can be utilized by anyone in analyzing why retail is at a serious crossroads when it comes to growth. Tayib moved us faster into how and why I think StockX is one of the best third party e-commerce platforms to be created.

In the Amazon chapter where I discussed how my entire store was wiped out by a glitch on the back end, I didn't explain what had to be done when I created a listing on Amazon. If a product already exists on Amazon, a marketplace owner has to use the pictures and information presented in the original listing. The problem is the listing could have the incorrect picture and the information and description of the shoe could be wrong. This creates an issue for the marketplace seller and can lead to returns, which it did. When the listing is wrong the marketplace seller has to create the listing from scratch. A seller can spend twenty minutes creating a listing only to encounter an older product that Amazon forces the new listing to be aligned with. Time is precious and Amazon requires a lot of time because the listing process is inefficient. On Amazon if the seller doesn't have all of the information for the product they can't sell that shoe, which isn't a bad thing. I actually thought this was one of the reasons Amazon was better than eBay. If the product was counterfeit chances are the UPC code was wrong so the seller couldn't list the shoe. The problem was if you bought a shoe directly from Nike and Nike used an old UPC code, which happens, the seller has to write Amazon, send a picture of the box label and the receipt and Amazon has to adjust the listing for the new product. This can take 24 hours, which is frustrating when a shoe is a new release and could sell out quickly. I do have to add that Amazon has a "Have One To Sell" feature, but even that has flaws.

Here are the steps for creating a listing on Amazon:

1. Find the correct category. There are about seven windows to click through before you find the correct category.
2. Once you've selected the category a new window opens. In that window there are eight tabs (Vital Info, Variations, Offer, Compliance, Images, Description, Keywords, More Details). Each of these tabs has an extensive amount of information to complete.
3. The Images tab isn't as straightforward as snapping a picture and posting. The images have to be a minimum of 1000 pixels on one side and the pics have to be white backgrounds; not off white or slightly grey, bright white. If there isn't a picture the listing won't show up. If the picture is slightly grey the product listing will be suppressed. The product description tab allows the seller to list any product flaws. The problem is the listing doesn't remain the way you create it.

It takes about 20 minutes to actually create a listing for one style. It takes even longer if pictures need editing. Remember when I said Amazon forced me to recreate over 500 listings? This is why I finally gave up. The process on Kixify is shorter and more efficient. The process on eBay can be decreased because you can duplicate older listings or use a template. On eBay and Amazon the perfect listing can be created, but if the marketplace seller doesn't have any feedback the listing doesn't rank as high and can be overlooked.

StockX offers a seamless selling process. This is one of the major reasons the platform could begin to expand and offer more items. The company has a team of employees that create the product. They post pictures and offer a description. If the shoes have older models they are distinguished by Style Code and if a seller has the shoe, they only have to check and see if there is an offer available. The seller doesn't have to take any pictures at all.

One of the biggest issues with selling on third party marketplaces is customer service. I retained a 5 star rating on Amazon for every year I was a seller. That rating is still there although I no longer list products on Amazon. Although I retained a very high seller rating, this didn't prevent numerous questions about authenticity or customers asking for decreased pricing. In the resale world we refer to the people writing as *lowballers*. You can spend an extra 10-15 minutes per day writing back and forth with a potential buyer who is asking for more pictures. I do a video of every shoe that I sell. I once had a customer on eBay write and ask for pictures. I gave the buyer a link to the video. The customer still wrote back and asked for pictures…

StockX isn't all roses. The team updating the shoe listings on the website don't respond quickly to submissions of shoes that aren't listed. I bought about 30 pairs of Saucony and ASICS for fifteen bucks a pop. I didn't take the time to check if the shoes were available on StockX prior to buying the shoes. I couldn't pass up the deal. StockX has a submission form so I submitted the shoes every few days and none of the models I submitted were added to the database. I understand that some shoes don't sell quickly and it takes man hours to add footwear and pictures, but this is a considerable flaw for the company. After a month I moved the shoes to my eBay shop and sold all of the models. Although this is an issue, customer service for a seller isn't bad at all with StockX.

I mentioned in an earlier chapter *chargebacks*. If I go back ten years I actually lost an eBay store because a customer claimed the shoes they bought from me were fakes. I wrote an entire series about this on my site. The irony of the buyer making this claim, he was selling my shoe on his eBay store at a higher price and when he couldn't sell them after thirty days, he wanted his money back.

StockX has eliminated issues with chargebacks. When a seller accepts an offer in some instances a message will appear explaining that there was a problem with the buyer's credit card. The seller never has to worry about a chargeback or a claim. This creates the perfect seller's platform, but in doing so the platform has truly turned everyone into a reseller which has created a huge conflict in the sneaker resale community. There are complaints about sellers undercutting each other, but these complaints are nonsensical.

StockX is a delivery system, not the seller. If prices are low it's because the buyer isn't as interested in the product, or the seller can afford to sell the product at lower prices. StockX is truly the world's first retail open market and while traditional retail isn't talking about it, the site has already disrupted both eBay and Amazon to a small extent and I predict that if the company adjusts a few details many sellers on eBay and Amazon will transition to StockX. I don't hesitate to say that if tomorrow StockX decided to make electronics available, *Best Buy* would feel the tremors.

I have to repeat though, the platform has made everyone a reseller and if you remember watching the movie *The Incredibles*, the antagonist named Syndrome wanted to make everyone "super" because in doing so no one would be "super". Turning everyone into a sneaker reseller flattens out the market, right? Not really.

Chapter 26

Inadvertent Support of 3rd Party?

In 2005 I could walk into the local Nike Clearance Store and find Retro 11s and racks upon racks of shoes. There were three of us back then who were buying large quantities of kicks; a lady from Kentucky and another guy from Arkansas. Today you can walk in and there are at least 20 people purchasing multiple pairs from Nike. This speaks towards an issue that is problematic for brick and mortar locations. I stated earlier that resale has traditionally taken place with buyers visiting Foot Locker, Finish Line and other chains. A seller who lives near a Nike Clearance or Factory Store can create a serious stream of income without ever setting foot inside of those retail locations. Nike has become an indirect supplier of third party. There have been weekends where I've visited local malls on what used to be major release days for Jordan Retro models and now no one is showing up. The reason for this is twofold:

1. Stores are using launch apps to prevent issues at retail. This has created an issue where store managers feel trapped between making their daily goals and waiting for buyers to show up. The registration in the app has created less demand because the person who wins the online raffle knows they don't have to rush to pick up their pair. The customer who isn't used to signing up via an app and still visits the store on the day of release can't buy the shoes. The store manager has to tell the customer that they can't sell the shoe until 3 or 6pm. The reservation allows for buyer's remorse and it creates frustration for managers looking to sell the shoes.
2. Every weekend if a person lives near a Nike Clearance or Factory Store, Nike launches either a 20% off or 30% off sale. They also offer incentives like $25-50 off purchases of 100 dollars that can be used in conjunction with the discounts. The lines inside of Nike Factory and Clearance

> Stores are typically 25 people deep and the stores have to use Crowd Control Stanchions to snake the line to the register.

This question has to be asked, "Is Nike's Consumer Direct Offense inadvertently or intentionally bolstering the third party marketplace?" If the answer is *inadvertent*, then what can traditional retailers do to fight this? If the answer is intentional, how long is it before Nike creates brand registries with third party companies like GOAT, StockX, Grailed and Poshmark; especially since the *price per transaction* on those platforms is much higher than brick and mortar businesses who have accounts with the brand. Foot Locker's recent investment into GOAT Group actually subverted Nike potentially doing this which is incredible to think about.

Tayib gave the number of shoes I sold in the previous chapter. What he didn't have was the gross amount of money I made selling via StockX. That total for 2018 was **$583,244**. If the holiday season hadn't disrupted shipping slightly, the total would have easily been $600,000. I listed all of the years I sold on Amazon for one reason, to show how much money was being left on the table by retailers. I'm listing this total for one reason, to establish that although there are more people entering resale than at any other time there is still a market for resale and StockX is an equivalent threat to traditional retail's revenue gross. If I'm utilizing brick and mortar and Nike as my inventory source and my revenue per transaction is $138.60, my small slice of the sneaker pie is performing at a better rate than most of the industry. Here is the thing, when I ship everyday there are about 15 other people dropping off boxes at the UPS store location I visit. Some drop off one or two boxes, others drop off fifteen to twenty. One guy drops off shoes that haven't released yet. It's an incredible thing to see, but I always consider that we have a professional NBA team here and some really famous rappers.

I've dropped off at other locations and the UPS person at those places scanning the boxes has always asked, "You sell shoes?" My response is "Why?" The person then states that I must be new because there are a lot of guys coming in and dropping off boxes with the same label. I sold 4200 pair of shoes and I'm not the biggest client of my local UPS location. That title belongs to three other sellers.

None of this would be possible if retail locations weren't working to drive traffic with sales and other promotional strategies. There are locations who have resorted to 'buy one get the second pair for a dollar' to clear inventory. There are some major chains that used 'buy one get one half off' tactics. Hibbett Sports was one of the major retail chains that did this. In the last year and a half, since Hibbett Sports launched its e-commerce business they haven't done a sale like this. That speaks volumes to the importance of a strong online presence.

These promotional tactics wouldn't happen if retail locations stopped relying solely on Google Adwords to acquire customers. None of this would happen if retail locations had in place something that required their employees to be as knowledgeable as possible about the products they are selling. Actually, I'm wrong… resale would exist because there will always be shoes that can't be purchased by some person somewhere. What I'm talking about is decreasing the amount of money left on the table at retail.

Chapter 27

StockX is Already Changing

StockX is on the precipice of disrupting resale in every market if they begin to adjust and make some changes. They have considerable opportunities that they could use to add revenue, but implementing those strategies could remove the simplicity of the platform. The biggest option the service has is eventually shifting towards brick and mortar as a seller; they actually made a small move towards this with a recent 'pop-up' store.

If StockX does what they recently did at Christmas in New York I 2018, they could expedite the time it takes to authenticate products. One of the main issues for StockX right now is the time it takes for the transaction from beginning to end:

- The seller has to pack then ship the shoes to StockX.
- StockX has to authenticate the shoes and repackage the pair to ship them to the buyer.

This creates a seven day turnaround for a buyer to get their product. Amazon has built an entire business around their speed in shipping. StockX slows down the sneaker buying process, but in doing so the buyer can rest easy knowing that the shoes are authentic. The irony is that the shoes Tayib and I sell are located in physical locations that offer *stock locating* and have online stores with the same products at or below retail.

When you really think about how StockX works it becomes apparent why CEOs of traditional retail don't think about these new third party sites as threats. There isn't any real ownership by third party retail. All the third party retail platform has is their delivery system and I think StockX is more efficient than Amazon for footwear sales. I say that the platform is a disruptive force with considerable room for growth, but it is also a very fragile business. I will discuss this a bit later.

Earlier in this book I quoted a visitor to my site describing his shopping experience of buying a shoe he had coveted since his youth. He bought the shoe for above retail. He didn't take the time to visit Foot Locker.com. Once Nike sold out, he left Nike's site and went straight to StockX. The third party sites are garnering the same amount of website traffic. This means that customers aren't looking online at traditional retail for premium products. They are looking at third party e-commerce sites. StockX realizes this and they are adjusting. The popup store was an interesting experiment for the digitally native business, but what exactly did StockX do at their popup?

How can an online platform that doesn't carry any products host a popup store? The popup store was for authenticating shoes and paying out to the seller immediately. The 'payout' from StockX happens via PayPal. A new seller has to wait until after the shoes are authenticated before they receive their payout. An experienced seller who has reached level 4, the highest level for sellers on StockX, gets their payout within 24 hours of dropping off the item at the UPS store.

The StockX popup, in my opinion, was a measuring stick for a retail play. As I said this isn't an analysis of StockX, but I can't help but explain why the ability for StockX to truly disrupt online traditional sneaker retail and other third party companies lies in this popup store.

Chapter

28

StockX vs Amazon Part 2

The popup allowed StockX to monitor foot traffic and interest in visiting a StockX door. Consider if they had reached out to all of their level 4 sellers and asked them if they wanted to utilize StockX as a physical shop? Sellers could have chosen to ship their footwear to StockX in a similar fashion to sellers utilizing *Fulfillment by Amazon*. That popup could have been a storefront and authentication center; placing StockX on a trajectory similar to GOAT. GOAT is already ahead of StockX in this way. The acquisition of Flight Club by GOAT was a genius move which allowed GOAT to transition from digital to brick and mortar. Could this be in the future of StockX? Possibly… the platform has already, in my opinion, made itself the elite resale platform in tech.

StockX has gotten rid of the multiple steps of resale. There is a reason I was able to generate over half a million dollars on StockX. I already had a system in place from my time on Amazon. What I was missing with Amazon was access to my capital to purchase all the time. When you consider I sold 4,270 pair of shoes and that in 2018 I created over 400 Authentic Verification videos for my YouTube channel, I sold multiple pairs of over 400 shoes. If I was still on Amazon the man hours in creating listings to sell a product would have been 400 x 20 Minutes, or 8000 minutes. That's 133 hours of time that I regained because StockX has removed many of the barriers to resale.

Both eBay and Amazon can create headaches via chargebacks and fraudulent transactions. StockX has a check in place that prevents a card from being processed if the details for the buyer aren't correct. The following is a message StockX sends when they catch a fraudulent transaction:

> Our Fraud Prevention Team caught an issue on your recent transaction due to suspicious activity with the buyer. Please DO NOT SHIP your item!
>
> We have listed your Ask for the Air More Uptempo Chrome White (W), size 8.5W.
>
> We apologize for the inconvenience, but the good news is that we caught it early. Even better news is that you don't have to deal with this kind of stuff - that's what we do.

Neither Amazon or eBay has a fraud protection policy in place that is preventive.

On Amazon, eBay and other third party platforms seller protection exists, but it's often a one sided process in favor of the buyer. The buyer can return a shoe or claim that the item shipped is fake which creates a lot of time spent e-mailing and working through claims and cases. StockX has created a platform that does not allow for buyer's remorse. Once a person who is offering the shoe (watch, handbag, etc) has an offer that they are willing to accept, they are taken through three windows confirming that they are certain of the transaction being made. There are two radio buttons before the seller completes the transaction. Once the offer is accepted, the transaction can't be cancelled. There are exceptions in some cases, but the seller will be charged fees if they cancel.

I didn't keep track of the number of returns I had on StockX this year, but it wasn't more than 30 pair returned. That's less than a 1% return rate. I would have placed an exclamation point, but it is clear this is unlike any sales platform in business. Many of the shoes returned I resold because there wasn't really anything wrong with the shoe other than the fact that someone had tried the shoes on and the outsole was dirty.

Many of these returns could have been prevented. StockX has the ability to earn more revenue by offering a cleaning service in lieu of processing returns. I'm not being asked to analyze and discuss how the platform can improve, but I have to bring attention to how many times I simply got the shoe back, took my toothbrush and hot, soapy water and cleaned the shoe. I then went back to the website within ten minutes of the return arriving and resold the same pair on the platform.

The company could recapture both man-hours and add a considerable amount of revenue with a shoe cleaning service. Sellers would also become a bit more efficient and aware of the items they are sending. I sometimes fail to check the shoes I buy because I'm shipping multiple pairs each day and they are coming directly from licensed retailers. My inconsistency in checking my shoes offers a chance to capture more revenue.

The other shoes that returned from StockX were because I made the error of sending a mismatch or I had the incorrect box. In almost every instance of a return I was at fault.

In comparison, on Amazon for every 10 pair of shoes I sold, 3 pair returned. Returns on Amazon became so rampant that I would wake up every morning dreading logging in to Seller Central. My beard turned grey, lol. Seriously, Amazon Seller Central as a platform created constant stress and tension. The threat of a review was constant and customers knew this and attempted to hold it over the head of the seller often. Many times when someone left a review it was a product review and not feedback on the service offered. This meant that I had to spend time writing Amazon to have feedback removed because I didn't want my sales to be affected. Amazon would also flag the Seller Account for being below standards. The morning routine on Amazon consisted of waking up early and grabbing my Kindle, logging into Seller Central and looking at the dashboard widgets to see if someone had written an e-mail, requested a return, or if the chargeback or case link was highlighted with a number.

A question I've continuously asked myself throughout my year on StockX was, "Why would a buyer use a platform where they can't make a return?" I spent so much time as a seller on Amazon I made an observation; a lot of customers are ordering from Amazon because returns are free, so they can try on the product and send it back without any issues. This has created a customer that is less thoughtful about their ordering process. That ease in buying is a problem for companies not named Amazon. My margins were too small to ship and then provide free shipping for the return. I had to implement a restocking fee and state it clearly in my e-mails. This worked, but it also required explaining in detail when I processed the refund why the amount was less the original total. It didn't matter that I gave the refund instructions in the original return acceptance e-mail. As Amazon began to force free returns on the Marketplace, it became increasingly difficult to apply a restocking fee. The restocking fee was critical because the value of shoes sold above retail fluctuated. Honestly, the majority of customers on Amazon realized that the price was cheaper in other locations after buying on Amazon. StockX may take longer to ship, but the platform has completely removed buyer's remorse; which is an amazing accomplishment.

Chapter 29

3rd Party Is No Longer 'Hype'

I stated that my sales in 2017 while testing StockX were all at the premium end of sales. In 2017 I only sold 85 pair of shoes for a total of 14,500 dollars. That's an average price of 170.00 per pair. As I mentioned earlier my initial perception of StockX was that the platform was for hypebeast and people looking for Yeezy, limited release Jordan Brand items and hard to find kicks. I don't use bots and I don't have connects here in Memphis. I use what I call my "route" to buy shoes. During the week I visit at least 4 locations per day. My goal is to spend about 4 hours total on reselling kicks. I choose stores that are in close proximity. It helps a ton when I can visit a mall which will usually have four locations in one stop. I also drive up to 1.5 hours away on certain days and once a month I will drive 2-3 hours away and make my shopping a day trip to other cities. A bit of a diversion here, when I do a day trip I typically visit a locally sourced restaurant and take pics and write a review for my CBP website. I'm in the process of rebuilding the site after it was hacked, but I'm adding this because it explains that my days aren't completely dominated by sneakers. This also tells those reading that the sneaker hunt provides more opportunities to create content for engagement.

If I stuck with my assessment of StockX from 2017 I would have thought that the platform was only for high end/hyped kicks. This would have led to this book carrying a completely different point of view. StockX operating at the premium end of the footwear spectrum is not a real threat to traditional retail at all. 2018 changed my perception and what became clear was that StockX is not just for selling high end sneakers but also for low end sneakers. Here is data showing the breakdown in sales by price. Remember this is data from one seller and can be utilized to create a micro to macro comparison. The information below shows pairs sold in 2018 that were in process to be paid in January 2nd; the number differs from the 4,208 I used as the official number in my year end video on YouTube and the number I've used in a number of locations in this book.

Number of Shoes Sold	Price Range	% Percentage of Sales
955	$30.00 to $100.00	22.37
1836	$100.00 to $150.00	43
1083	$151.00 to $200.00	25.36
288	$201.00 to $250.00	6.75
109	$251.00 to $849.00	2.53
Total: 4270		

I failed to request my CSV from StockX at the end of 2017 which hurts this discussion a bit, but to move from 170 to an average of $583,244 / 4270 = $136.59 hints at what the chart above establishes. StockX has shifted demographics. The site is no longer pulling in people because of shoes that have hit resale, or are limited; the site is capturing sales on a considerable amount of "non-sneakerhead" shoes listed on the site. I happen to think the least expensive shoes sold could be higher from 30-100, but the site does not list a lot of shoes. Very often I can walk around a Nike store and find kicks I know someone would buy and because the pair isn't listed on StockX I passed them on to other sellers and people in the store. This happens at every location I visit. Unlike Amazon, eBay and Kixify, a seller can't create a listing on StockX. A seller can only suggest a listing and very often the suggestion is never added.

Take for instance the Fila Disruptor that Tayib sold via other third party platforms. Tayib was selling that model throughout 2018. I couldn't sell the shoe because it wasn't available although I had submitted the item to StockX on several occasions. The shoe is finally available, but the model has cooled significantly. This is a serious issue for StockX and an opening for retail accounts. If stores produced as much content as StockX and increased engagement in a similar fashion many of the shoes sold on StockX wouldn't ever reach the platform. StockX exists primarily because of the authentication service but the site has transcended the realm of hyped sneakers and now has become a place for sneaker steals and in many ways functions as an outlet market.

Retailers who have decided to utilize sales and promo as a means to drive engagement and foot traffic are moving towards a point where StockX is eventually going to *eat up* all of their margins. How is this possible? Margins for traditional retail that operates "by the book" are at risk due to the combination of direct to consumer, the promotional market, and brick and mortar attempting to get ahead of the market by selling early. This last item should be a point of discussion. On every third party marketplace there are an abundance of sales made prior to a shoe being released. The only way this can happen is if,

1. Stolen shoes are entering the market.
2. Retailers are selling shoes prior to release date.

By whatever means, sneakers are entering the digital marketplace prior to the established release day for traditional wholesale accounts carrying and releasing the product. Let me make this sentence clear: someone is selling kicks super early and it's messing up the market. If I was from Oakland I would write that I'm *hella* frustrated because early releases no longer build the market up, it tears it down. At one point, prior to StockX and GOAT, people who had access to shoes early primarily sold the shoes wholesale and sites like Flight Club, or Power Seller eBay accounts resold the shoes at higher prices. Those higher prices elevated the value and this is what led to long lines on release days. The perception of value was motivation and fueled desires for the kicks.

Now that there are more outlets for purchasing footwear early and the walls of resale have been taken down, the people who get kicks early are selling the shoes themselves. The result is simply cause and effect. There isn't a middle man, well there is a middle man, but that added financial layer that traditionally insulated the price at above retail is gone and with it so are the margins for traditional retail.

Chapter 30

Know Your Enemy

How does StockX reduce margins for traditional retail? StockX doesn't follow protocol. Tayib sent me an e-mail during our experiment. It was in regard to the Air Jordan 1 Sports Illustrated. The letter Tayib wrote was around December 14th, 2018. This is what he wrote, "Yesterday when I check(ed) aj1 sports illustrated 1,433 were sold on stockx. Stockx can contribute to the perception that a product is not desirable, by allowing the item to be sold prior to its release date for up to 30 to 49% lower than its suggested retail price."

Tayib's point about desirability is interesting. He was writing from the standpoint that as a reseller he couldn't capitalize on the Sports Illustrated because the shoe in certain sizes was selling below retail when the release date arrived. In the past a reseller could pick up pairs from Foot Locker or their local sneaker shop and flip them for a small profit. StockX in many ways has removed that opportunity.

In the previous chapter I explained that shoes are entering the market prior to their release date. The official day of release for the Sports Illustrated Air Jordan 1 was December 27th, 2018. By the day of release StockX had sold over 2000 pair and while some of the smaller sizes are currently selling above retail, the average resale price on StockX is currently 153.00, below retail. More troublesome for retailers is this information on the breakdown of available shoes for purchase for the Air Jordan 1 Sports Illustrated:

Size 10.5 – $158.00

Size 11 – $152.00

Size 11.5 – $152.00

Size 12 – $135.00

Size 12.5 – $145.00

Size 13 – $135.00

Size 14 – $148.00

Consumers are becoming more aware that the shoes are available below retail so what happens to traditional retailers carrying the model? Almost every wholesale account still has the shoe in stock in larger sizes. This was a shoe that should have sold out quickly. Instead the value of the shoe on StockX has plummeted in sizes above size 10. The Air Jordan 1 Sports Illustrated provides some confirmation that when a shoe is made available early and does not carry significant resale value it shapes the retail market negatively. StockX as a business still earns revenue on the items sold on the site, so the resale price is of little consequence as the business still earns its transaction fees. Retailers have to begin discounting to compete.

The problem is when retailers drop prices to try and compete with online stores, they lose margins. When retailers drop prices to compete with other retail outlets, they lose margins. When retailers are in cities with a Nike Clearance Store the price drop has become insignificant because Nike Clearance and Factory stores now carry similar products. The retailer has to drop prices even more to clear out inventory.

The retailer is in a battle and the castle is surrounded. Because Nike would rather sell directly to the consumer than via retailers; Nike has indirectly led to the rise of third party because everyone is discounting as opposed to finding a way to fuel interest in the products being carried; which brings this entire discussion full circle.

Third party should only exist as a means of getting hard to find sneakers. Third party, however, has drifted into general release products readily available at brick and mortar because access in certain areas is limited and because traditional retailers have relied on marketing departments unwilling to utilize the new digital playbook in promoting their websites.

At the beginning of this book I discussed the Nike Flash Sale and explained that the goal of the sale was to acquire customers and move those new customers into Nike's digital channel. Take a moment to realize that Nike is now offering weekly sales at their Factory and Clearance locations. These sales are 20-30% off of already reduced prices. Customers are signing up for Nike.com and downloading the app at the register. When they purchase the product their receipt is sent to their e-mail and a follow up e-mail arrives announcing the latest Nike release. When the next sale begins an e-mail is sent.

While this book has been about Nike, every brand is working on direct-to-consumer strategies and they are all attempting to increase the number of brick and mortar stores, as well as capture e-commerce sales.

Third party platforms are the beneficiaries of retailers unwilling to commit to a long-term strategy in marketing. Sneaker lifestyle websites write constantly about the next sneaker releasing. When sites like Complex, Hypebeast and Highsnobiety know a release is on the horizon they feature digital shops like StockX and GOAT. These third party platforms work with and through sneaker culture websites to announce that the product is already available on their sites way ahead of the release date.

Sneaker culture websites are controlling search on any new product dropping requiring traditional brick and mortar to run Sponsored Product Ads to be placed before the fold on *search and shop pages* on Google and Bing. Creating a loop for retailers:

- Buy shoe from brand
- Get shoe in stores
- Send an e-mail 24 hours before release
- Make a splash page for release day
- Run ads to generate interest
- Reduce price to get rid of inventory
- Repeat

While Third Party and Sneaker Culture websites, 6 months ahead of time:

- Discuss leaked pictures
- Update leaked pictures
- Discuss the athlete's latest endeavor
- Discuss the multitude of releases by the brand
- Get confirmation of the actual release
- Show pictures of the actual release
- Link to the brand website
- Talk about the designer
- Talk about the event surrounding the release
- Link to a third party platform
- Repeat

Tayib and I didn't go to school for marketing. We didn't go to school for business. Tayib and I are educators who have been in the sneaker business for a combined 25+ years. In 2015 we understood the mistakes we made in establishing our businesses and we adjusted. Everyone, every business, is now a media company.

When Sun Tzu wrote ‘know your enemy,” if he was discussing the impending war between retail, brands and third party he would have made the same comment he made, “become your enemy.” If Nike is leading sneaker retail by shifting to direct to consumer and Amazon is adding private labels, while third party is expanding into brick and mortar, retailers have to become all of the above.

Made in the USA
San Bernardino, CA
22 February 2019